Fruit

by Elizabeth Baird

A Madison Press Book

ISBN-10: 1-895892-93-7
ISBN-13: 978-1-895892-93-2

EDITORIAL DIRECTOR: Hugh Brewster
SUPERVISING EDITOR: Wanda Nowakowska
PROJECT EDITOR: Beverley Sotolov
EDITORIAL ASSISTANCE: Beverley Renahan
PRODUCTION DIRECTOR: Susan Barrable
PRLDUCTION COORDINATOR: Donna Chong
BOOK DESIGN AND LAYOUT: Gordon Sibley Design Inc.
COVER DESIGN: Sharon Foster
COVER PHOTOGRAPHY: Gentl & Hyers/FoodPix/Jupiterimages
COLOR SEPARATION: Colour Technologies
ADVISORY BOARD: Elizabeth Baird, Bonnie Baker Cowan,
Anna Hobbs, Caren King

Cook's Own: Fruit
was produced by

MADISON PRESS BOOKS
1000 Yonge Street, Suite 200
Toronto, Ontario
Canada M4W 2K2
www.madisonpressbooks.com

Printed in China by Lotus Printing Inc.

Contents

Introduction

Fruit is a feast for our senses through all seasons of the year. Strawberries tumbling into a basket send up irresistible perfumes of summer. Golden peaches at harvest fairly burst with sweetness when you bite into them. And when cold weather drops the curtain on three seasons of amazing abundance, bushels heaped with crisp red, russet and green apples celebrate the finale, before summer's bounty is preserved as jams, jellies and relishes you can enjoy all year round.

All fruit is important. Packed with vitamins and fiber, it is the easiest-to-like package of nutrition possible, a refreshing way to eat for vitality.

But let's own up to our pleasures. There's more to fruit than health considerations. Even the most health-conscious among us give in to a decadent fruit cheesecake sometimes.

Fruit plays a starring role in the kitchen, as the more than 100 recipes in *Cook's Own: Fruit* show. When the harbinger of spring, those pink shoots of rhubarb, appear in the frigid garden, thoughts stray to moist rhubarb coffee cakes. Summer berries inspire the fools, semifreddos, salad medleys, homemade ice creams, sorbets and fresh fruit sauces that make reputations every time they're served. For fancy occasions, fruit folds into tortes and cakes, or is whizzed into tall charlottes or trifles to impress. For modest mornings, it's the pancakes studded with blueberries or the muffins perked up with chopped clementines that are the great wake-up calls. And for those of you who want to savor the wonders of nectarines, plums and peaches long after the first snowfall, *Cook's Own: Fruit* shows wonderful ways to preserve them.

Cook's Own: Fruit is the indispensable practical planner for cooking, baking and preserving the fruits of all four seasons, with helpful hints for shopping and storage, plus make-ahead suggestions and cooking tips. Enjoy *Cook's Own: Fruit* for its welcome to the inspired world of fruit.

Elizabeth Baird

Cobblers, Crisps and Puddings

Call this comfort food on a spoon! With bubbling fruit fillings under a crunchy blanket of crumble or biscuit, warm-from-the-oven cobblers and crisps are one of life's little pleasures — and perfect for any day of the week.

Peach and Raspberry Cobbler ▶

Keep the fruits of August in mind for this high-fiber, lightened-up cobbler.

Per serving: about
- 330 calories
- 7 g fat
- high source of fiber
- 6 g protein
- 64 g carbohydrate

4 cups	thickly sliced pitted peaches (about 6 large)	1 L
2 cups	raspberries	500 mL
2 tbsp	lemon juice	25 mL
1/4 cup	granulated sugar	50 mL
2 tbsp	all-purpose flour	25 mL
1/4 tsp	cinnamon	1 mL
	BISCUIT TOPPING	
1-1/2 cups	all-purpose flour	375 mL
1/3 cup	granulated sugar	75 mL
1 tsp	baking powder	5 mL
1/2 tsp	baking soda	2 mL
Pinch	salt	Pinch
3 tbsp	butter, cubed	50 mL
2/3 cup	buttermilk	150 mL
1/2 tsp	vanilla	2 mL

● In bowl, toss together peaches, raspberries and lemon juice. Combine sugar, flour and cinnamon; sprinkle over fruit, tossing to coat well. Spoon into 8-inch (2 L) square baking dish; level top.

● BISCUIT TOPPING: In bowl, stir together flour, 1/4 cup (50 mL) of the sugar, baking powder, baking soda and salt. With pastry blender or two knives, cut in butter until crumbly. Pour in buttermilk and vanilla; stir with fork until soft dough forms.

● Turn out onto lightly floured surface; pat into 1/2-inch (1 cm) thickness. Using cookie cutter, cut out rounds, rerolling scraps once. Arrange over fruit. Sprinkle with remaining sugar.

● Bake in 375°F (190°C) oven for about 35 minutes or until bubbly and topping is golden and no longer doughy underneath. Makes 6 servings.

TIPS
● If you use frozen raspberries, increase the baking time by 5 to 10 minutes.
● Here's a quick way to cut biscuits. Pat out dough into a large square to fit the baking dish, then cut into 6 or 12 blocks. Arrange over fruit.

Maple Apple Pudding

Old-fashioned pleasure is what this pudding is all about. Buttermilk drop biscuits top a layer of maple-sweetened apples.

Per serving: about
- 555 calories
- 9 g fat
- 4 g protein
- 66 g carbohydrate

4 cups	sliced peeled apples	1 L
2/3 cup	maple syrup	150 mL
1/3 cup	raisins	75 mL
1 cup	all-purpose flour	250 mL
1/4 cup	granulated sugar	50 mL
1-1/2 tsp	baking powder	7 mL
1/2 tsp	baking soda	2 mL
1/4 tsp	salt	1 mL
1/4 cup	butter, softened	50 mL
1/2 cup	buttermilk	125 mL
1	egg	1
1 tsp	vanilla	5 mL

● In saucepan, bring apples and maple syrup to boil; reduce heat and simmer for 3 minutes or until softened. Add raisins. Pour into greased 8-inch (2 L) square baking dish.

● In bowl, combine flour, sugar, baking powder, baking soda and salt; with pastry blender or two knives, cut in butter until crumbly. Whisk together buttermilk, egg and vanilla; pour over flour mixture, stirring just until combined.

● Drop by large spoonfuls onto apple mixture. Bake in 350°F (180°C) oven for 30 minutes or until cake tester inserted in center comes out clean. Makes 6 servings.

Cookie Cobbler

4 cups	sliced peeled apples	1 L
1-1/2 cups	frozen blueberries	375 mL
1-1/2 cups	frozen raspberries	375 mL
1/3 cup	granulated sugar	75 mL
1/4 cup	apple juice	50 mL
2 tbsp	cornstarch	25 mL
1/4 tsp	cinnamon	1 mL
	COOKIE TOPPING	
2/3 cup	butter, softened	150 mL
1/2 cup	granulated sugar	125 mL
1	egg	1
1 tsp	vanilla	5 mL
1 cup	all-purpose flour	250 mL
1/2 tsp	baking powder	2 mL
1/4 tsp	cinnamon	1 mL
Pinch	salt	pinch

● In bowl, toss together apples, blueberries, raspberries, sugar, apple juice, cornstarch and cinnamon. Spread in 11- x 7-inch (2 L) baking dish.

● COOKIE TOPPING: In bowl, beat butter with sugar until fluffy; beat in egg and vanilla. Stir together flour, baking powder, cinnamon and salt; gradually stir into butter mixture. Drop by rounded tablespoonfuls (15 mL) onto fruit mixture.

● Bake in 375°F (190°C) oven for about 55 minutes or until fruit is tender and topping is cooked through and no longer doughy underneath. Makes 6 servings.

A *drop-cookie batter makes a novel topping for apples and berries. Serve this year-round with either fresh or frozen berries. When using fresh, reduce the cooking time by 5 to 10 minutes.*

Per serving: about
- 470 calories
- 4 g protein
- 22 g fat
- 67 g carbohydrate
- high source of fiber

Five-Fruit Crisp

5 cups	sliced peeled apples	1.25 L
1-1/2 cups	dried cranberries	375 mL
5 cups	sliced pears	1.25 L
1/2 cup	orange or apple juice	125 mL
1 tsp	finely grated lemon rind	5 mL
2 tbsp	lemon juice	25 mL
1 tsp	cinnamon	5 mL
1/2 tsp	grated nutmeg	2 mL
	TOPPING	
3/4 cup	all-purpose flour	175 mL
1/2 cup	packed brown sugar	125 mL
1/2 cup	butter, softened	125 mL
1/2 cup	slivered almonds	125 mL
1/2 cup	rolled oats	125 mL

● In 13- x 9-inch (3 L) baking dish, layer apples, then cranberries, then pears. Stir together orange juice, lemon rind and juice, cinnamon and nutmeg; drizzle over fruit.

● TOPPING: In bowl, combine flour with sugar. With pastry blender or two knives, cut in butter until crumbly. Stir in almonds and oats; sprinkle evenly over fruit.

● Bake in 350°F (180°C) oven for about 50 minutes or until topping is crisp and golden and fruit is tender and bubbly. Let cool slightly. Makes 12 servings.

VARIATION
● SMALL-CROWD FIVE-FRUIT CRISP: Divide all ingredients in half, using 1/2 cup (125 mL) flour in topping. Bake in 8-inch (2 L) square baking dish for about 40 minutes. Makes 6 servings.

T*his homey blend of apples, dried cranberries and pears makes a quick dessert during the festive season — but it's so delicious you'll want to serve it for many occasions, big or small.*

Per serving: about
- 310 calories
- 4 g protein
- 11 g fat
- 53 g carbohydrate
- high source of fiber

Apple Oat Crisp

The yin and yang of apple crisp lies in the thick layer of tart and tender fruit under a sweet and crunchy topping. Northern Spys, Spartans or Granny Smiths deliver for the apple layer.

Per each of 8 servings: about
• 240 calories • 2 g protein
• 7 g fat • 45 g carbohydrate

8 cups	sliced peeled tart apples (about 2-2/3 lb/1.35 kg)	2 L
1/4 cup	granulated sugar	50 mL
1/4 cup	apple juice	50 mL
1 tbsp	lemon juice	15 mL
	TOPPING	
2/3 cup	all-purpose flour	150 mL
2/3 cup	rolled oats	150 mL
1/3 cup	packed brown sugar	75 mL
1/2 tsp	cinnamon	2 mL
1/4 cup	butter, melted	50 mL

● In 8-inch (2 L) square baking dish, toss together apples, sugar and apple and lemon juices; level top.

● TOPPING: In bowl, toss together flour, oats, sugar and cinnamon; drizzle with butter, tossing with fork until combined. Sprinkle evenly over apples.

● Bake in 375°F (190°C) oven for about 45 minutes or until topping is crisp and filling is tender and bubbly. Let cool for 30 minutes. Makes 6 to 8 servings.

TIP: Old-fashioned large-flake rolled oats are best for a textured crisp topping.

Strawberry Rhubarb Crisp

Two summertime favorites take to the grill in an easy crisp that's perfect — and perfectly delicious! — during barbecue season. Bake the crisp in a covered grill at the same time as the main course, or beforehand if you like.

Per serving: about
• 305 calories • 3 g protein
• 9 g fat • 55 g carbohydrate

4 cups	sliced rhubarb	1 L
2 cups	sliced strawberries	500 mL
1 cup	packed brown sugar	250 mL
1/2 cup	rolled oats	125 mL
1/2 cup	all-purpose flour	125 mL
1/2 tsp	cinnamon	2 mL
1/4 cup	butter	50 mL

● In greased 8-inch (2 L) square metal cake pan, combine rhubarb, strawberries and 1/3 cup (75 mL) of the sugar; level top.

● In bowl, combine oats, flour, remaining sugar and cinnamon. With pastry blender or two knives, cut in butter until crumbly. Sprinkle evenly over fruit.

● Place pan on baking sheet on grill over medium heat (375°F/190°C); close lid and cook for 30 to 40 minutes or until bubbly and top is browned. Makes 6 servings.

TIP: Indoors, bake the crisp in a 375°F (190°C) oven for 30 to 40 minutes or until crisp and bubbly.

HANDY CRISP TOPPER

Once this topping mix is made up and waiting in the fridge, it's a breeze to assemble an apple, pear, peach or berry crisp.

2 cups	all-purpose flour	500 mL
2 cups	quick-cooking rolled oats	500 mL
1-1/3 cups	packed brown sugar	325 mL
1 tbsp	cinnamon	15 mL
1 tsp	nutmeg	5 mL

● In bowl, combine flour, oats, sugar, cinnamon and nutmeg. *(Mix can be refrigerated or frozen in airtight container for up to 2 months.)* Makes about 6 cups (1.5 L).

● For an 8-inch (2 L) square baking dish filled with lightly sweetened and moistened fruit, toss 1-1/4 cups (300 mL) of this mix with 1/3 cup (75 mL) melted butter until combined. For a change of taste, add 1/4 cup (50 mL) shredded coconut, slivered almonds or other chopped nuts to the mix.

Per 1/4 cup (50 mL) serving: about
• 115 calories • 2 g protein • 1 g fat • 25 g carbohydrate

Extra-Easy Apple Betty

10 cups	sliced peeled apples (about 3 lb/1.5 kg)	2.5 L
1/4 cup	apple juice	50 mL
2 cups	fine oatmeal cookie crumbs	500 mL
1/4 cup	butter, melted	50 mL
1/2 tsp	cinnamon	2 mL

● In large bowl, toss apples with apple juice; spread half of the mixture in 8-inch (2 L) square baking dish.

● Combine cookie crumbs, butter and cinnamon; sprinkle half over apples. Repeat layers.

● Bake in 375°F (190°C) oven for about 50 minutes or until apples are tender. Makes 6 servings.

A *"betty" is a layered fruit-and-crumb baked pudding. Oatmeal cookies — already sweetened — add to the convenience of this extra-easy dessert.*

Per serving: about
• 310 calories • 2 g protein
• 13 g fat • 48 g carbohydrate
• high source of fiber

Fruit Meringue

6 cups	quartered pitted prune plums	1.5 L
2 cups	pitted sour cherries	500 mL
Dash	almond extract	Dash
1/4 cup	granulated sugar	50 mL
2 tbsp	cornstarch	25 mL
	TOPPING	
3	egg whites	3
1/4 tsp	cream of tartar	1 mL
1/3 cup	granulated sugar	75 mL
Dash	almond extract	Dash

● In bowl, toss together plums, cherries and almond extract. Sprinkle with sugar and cornstarch; toss to coat evenly.

● Spoon into 8-inch (2 L) square baking dish; level top. Cover and bake in 375°F (190°C) oven for about 40 minutes or until fruit is very tender.

● TOPPING: Meanwhile, in bowl, beat egg whites with cream of tartar until soft peaks form. Beat in sugar, 1 tbsp (15 mL) at a time and adding almond extract with last addition, until stiff peaks form.

● Spoon topping over fruit, smoothing with back of spoon. Bake in 375°F (190°C) oven for about 10 minutes or until meringue is golden brown. Let cool to room temperature. Makes 6 to 8 servings.

I*nstead of a buttery crisp topping, this pudding is crowned with a low-fat, spoon-soft pillow of golden meringue.*

Per each of 8 servings: about
• 160 calories • 3 g protein
• 1 g fat • 37 g carbohydrate

Chocolate Banana Bread Pudding ▶

This sumptuous pudding features cubes of banana bread in baked custard with nuggets of truffle. Serve with Pitcher-Pouring Custard (p. 43), frozen yogurt or ice cream and a splash of Raspberry Coulis (p. 46).

Per serving: about
- 435 calories
- 11 g protein
- 26 g fat
- 47 g carbohydrate
- good source of iron

1/3 cup	whipping cream	75 mL
12 oz	bittersweet or semisweet chocolate, chopped	375 g
1/4 cup	butter	50 mL
3 cups	milk	750 mL
3	eggs	3
3	egg yolks	3
1 tsp	vanilla	5 mL
	BANANA BREAD	
1/2 cup	packed brown sugar	125 mL
1/4 cup	butter, melted	50 mL
2	eggs	2
1 cup	mashed bananas (about 3 small)	250 mL
1 tsp	vanilla	5 mL
2 cups	all-purpose flour	500 mL
2 tsp	baking powder	10 mL
1/2 tsp	baking soda	2 mL
1/2 tsp	salt	2 mL
1/2 cup	buttermilk	125 mL

● BANANA BREAD: In bowl, whisk sugar with butter; whisk in eggs, one at a time. Whisk in bananas and vanilla.

● Stir together flour, baking powder, baking soda and salt; stir into banana mixture alternately with buttermilk, making three additions of flour mixture and two of buttermilk. Scrape into greased 8- x 4-inch (1.5 L) loaf pan.

● Bake in 350°F (180°C) oven for about 1 hour or until tester inserted in center comes out clean. Let cool in pan on rack for 15 minutes. Remove from pan; let cool completely on rack. *(Bread can be wrapped in plastic wrap and stored for up to 1 day at room temperature or sealed in freezer bag and frozen for up to 2 weeks.)*

● Meanwhile, in small saucepan, heat cream, half of the chocolate and 1 tbsp (15 mL) of the butter over medium heat, stirring, until chocolate is melted. Scrape into bowl; let cool. *(Chocolate can be covered and refrigerated for up to 3 days.)*

● In saucepan, heat milk with remaining chocolate and butter over medium heat, whisking, until chocolate is melted. In bowl, whisk together eggs, egg yolks and vanilla; whisk in milk mixture. Let cool.

● Cut banana bread into cubes; spread half in greased 13- x 9-inch (3 L) baking dish. Drizzle evenly with half of the egg mixture. Cut solid chocolate mixture into cubes; sprinkle over bread. Top with remaining banana bread cubes; drizzle evenly with remaining egg mixture. Let stand for 5 minutes; press gently to moisten bread evenly.

● Bake in 350°F (180°C) oven for about 30 minutes or until knife inserted in center comes out clean. Makes 12 servings.

TIP: Inexpensive plastic squeeze bottles are indispensable when decorating dessert plates in the kitchen. A few dramatic squeezes of a raspberry coulis or chocolate over a pool of custard, for example, will turn a humble offering into a creative masterpiece!

Chocolate Banana Bread Pudding

Fruity Bread Pudding for Two

1 cup	cubed bread	250 mL
1/2 cup	chopped peeled apples	125 mL
1/4 cup	dried cranberries, cherries or chopped apricots	50 mL
1	egg	1
1/4 cup	granulated sugar	50 mL
1 tsp	vanilla	5 mL
1/2 cup	milk	125 mL
1 tsp	butter	5 mL
	Cinnamon	

● In lightly greased 2-cup (500 mL) baking dish, toss together bread, apples and cranberries.

● In small bowl, whisk together egg, sugar and vanilla. In small saucepan, heat milk with butter just until steaming; gradually whisk into egg mixture in slow, steady stream. Pour over bread mixture. Let stand for 5 minutes; press gently to moisten bread evenly. Sprinkle with cinnamon to taste.

● Bake in 350°F (180°C) oven for about 30 minutes or just until puffed and knife inserted in center comes out clean. Broil for about 2 minutes or until golden and crusty. Makes 2 servings.

Lightened-up comfort food such as this quick and easy bread pudding is perfectly in tune with today's tastes. For extra servings, simply double the recipe and bake in a larger dish.

Per serving: about
- 285 calories
- 6 g fat
- 7 g protein
- 51 g carbohydrate

Almond Baked Apples ▶

*Choose tart varieties —
Northern Spy or Idared —
if your taste runs to firmer,
more shapely apples.
If you prefer a softer texture,
Spartan, Cortland,
Gravenstein or Mac are
the best bet.*

Per serving: about
- 330 calories
- 2 g protein
- 10 g fat
- 63 g carbohydrate
- high source
  of fiber

1/2 cup	apple juice	125 mL
1/3 cup	liquid honey	75 mL
2 tbsp	butter	25 mL
1/4 tsp	grated nutmeg	1 mL
4	tart apples	4
1/4 cup	dried cranberries or raisins	50 mL
3 tbsp	toasted slivered almonds	50 mL
3 tbsp	cookie crumbs (ginger, sugar, graham)	50 mL

● In small saucepan, combine apple juice, honey, butter and nutmeg; bring to boil. Reduce heat and boil gently for 10 to 12 minutes or until thickened.

● Meanwhile, core apples almost to bottom, leaving base intact. Pare off 3/4-inch (2 cm) wide strip around core at top; trim base to level if necessary. Place in 8-inch (2 L) square baking dish.

● Pour juice mixture over apples. Cover and bake in 375°F (190°C) oven for about 45 minutes or until tender, basting twice.

● Combine cranberries, almonds and cookie crumbs; stuff into apple cavities. Baste with pan juices; bake for 5 minutes longer. Baste again before serving. Makes 4 servings.

Apricot and Raisin Rice Pudding

*There are two secrets to a
great rice pudding — using
short-grain rice, and slow-
cooking it in milk so the
grains swell and release their
starch to thicken the milk.
With this recipe, even 1% or
2% milk delivers luxurious
creaminess.*

Per serving: about
- 300 calories
- 10 g protein
- 5 g fat
- 55 g carbohydrate
- good source
  of calcium

3 cups	milk	750 mL
1/2 cup	short-grain rice	125 mL
1/4 cup	granulated sugar	50 mL
1/4 cup	raisins	50 mL
1/4 cup	chopped dried apricots	50 mL
1/4 tsp	salt	1 mL
1	egg	1
1 tsp	vanilla	5 mL
Pinch	each cinnamon and grated nutmeg	Pinch

● In heavy saucepan, bring milk and rice to boil. Reduce heat to low; cover and simmer very gently, stirring occasionally, for 15 minutes.

● Stir in sugar, raisins, apricots and salt; cover and simmer gently, stirring occasionally, for about 30 minutes or until rice is very tender.

● In bowl, beat egg; stir in 2 cups (500 mL) of the rice mixture. Stir egg mixture back into saucepan; remove from heat.

● Stir in vanilla, cinnamon and nutmeg. Cover and let cool for 30 minutes or just until warm. Makes 4 servings.

TIPS

● Rice pudding is just as good cold (it makes a quick and nutritious breakfast on the run), but it does thicken as it cools. Stir in a little extra milk to bring it to the consistency you enjoy.

● Dried fruits such as raisins, cranberries or chopped prunes, figs or dates can replace the apricots.

It's a Piece of Cake

Fruit and cake make a blissful union — whether it's a shower of summer berries on a decadent strawberry mousse cake or the tangy-sweet hit of rhubarb in a deliciously easy custard torte. Here's the very best of both!

White Chocolate Cheesecake with Fruit ▶

You need only a small slice of this divinely dense cheesecake — but be lavish with the fruit that tops and spills over each serving.

Per serving: about
- 435 calories
- 33 g fat
- 8 g protein
- 8 g carbohydrate

60	vanilla wafers (about 6 oz/175 g)	60
1/2 cup	butter, melted	125 mL
8 oz	white chocolate, coarsely chopped	250 g
1 cup	light cream	250 mL
3	pkg (8 oz/250 g each) cream cheese, softened	3
1/4 cup	granulated sugar	50 mL
4	eggs	4
2 tsp	vanilla	10 mL
3/4 cup	Raspberry Coulis (recipe, p. 46)	175 mL
4 cups	sliced fresh fruit and berries	1 L

● Grease bottom and side of 9-inch (2.5 L) springform pan. Line side with parchment paper. Set on large piece of foil; press foil against side of pan.

● In food processor, grind vanilla wafers to fine crumbs; add butter and blend until evenly moistened. Press onto bottom and 1/2 inch (1 cm) up side of prepared pan. Bake in 350°F (180°C) oven for 15 minutes or until golden brown at edges. Let cool on rack.

● Meanwhile, in bowl set over hot (not boiling) water, melt together white chocolate and cream; stir gently until smooth. Let cool to room temperature.

● In separate bowl, beat cream cheese with sugar until fluffy; beat in eggs, one at a time, beating well after each addition. Stir in white chocolate mixture and vanilla. Pour into cooled crust.

● Set pan in larger pan; pour in enough hot water to come 1 inch (2.5 cm) up sides. Bake in 325°F (160°C) oven for about 1 hour and 15 minutes or until center is just set and edge is slightly puffed. Remove from water bath and place on rack; remove foil and let cool completely. *(Cake can be covered and refrigerated for up to 2 days.)*

● Pool Raspberry Coulis on plates; place slice of cheesecake on coulis. Top with fruit. Makes 16 servings.

TIPS
● You can use 1-3/4 cups (425 mL) graham crumbs in place of vanilla wafers.
● Most cheesecakes are still slightly jiggly when done, but this one is quite firm and dense, so it will seem set. If jiggly, it is still underdone.

Raspberry-Glazed Lemon Cheesecake

Low-fat cottage cheese, yogurt and light cream cheese blend and bake into a fine cheesecake. Corn syrup, which replaces some of the butter in this lower-fat version of a typical crumb crust, adds a delightful crispness.

Per serving: about
- 275 calories
- 9 g fat
- 12 g protein
- 38 g carbohydrate

2 cups	plain yogurt	500 mL
1 cup	granulated sugar	250 mL
2 tbsp	lemon rind	25 mL
1/2 cup	lemon juice	125 mL
2 cups	1% or 2% cottage cheese	500 mL
8 oz	light cream cheese, cubed and softened	250 g
2	eggs	2
3	egg whites	3
1/4 cup	all-purpose flour	50 mL
1 tsp	vanilla	5 mL
	CRUST	
1 cup	graham cracker crumbs	250 mL
1 tbsp	butter, melted	15 mL
2 tbsp	corn syrup	25 mL
	RASPBERRY GLAZE	
1	pkg (10 oz/300 g) individually frozen raspberries, thawed	1
4 tsp	cornstarch	20 mL
2 tbsp	icing sugar	25 mL
4 tsp	lemon juice	20 mL

● Pour yogurt into cheesecloth-lined sieve set over bowl; cover and refrigerate to drain for at least 3 hours or until reduced to 1 cup (250 mL). Discard liquid.

● CRUST: Meanwhile, line bottom of 10-inch (3 L) springform pan with parchment paper. Center pan on large piece of foil; press foil to side of pan. Set aside.

● In food processor, mix crumbs with butter. Add corn syrup; blend until mixture starts to hold together. Press evenly onto bottom of prepared pan. Bake in 350°F (180°C) oven for 10 minutes.

● Meanwhile, in food processor, combine sugar and lemon rind and juice. Add cottage cheese; blend, scraping down side of bowl twice, for about 30 seconds or until no longer granular. With motor running, add drained yogurt and cream cheese; blend until combined. Add eggs, egg whites, flour and vanilla; blend until smooth. Pour over prepared crust.

● Set pan in larger pan; pour in enough hot water to come 1 inch (2.5 cm) up sides of pans. Bake in 325°F (160°C) oven for about 1-1/4 hours or until set around edge yet still jiggly in center. Turn oven off; quickly run knife around cake. Let stand in oven for 1 hour.

● Remove from larger pan and remove foil; let cool completely on rack. Cover and refrigerate for at least 8 hours or until thoroughly chilled. *(Cake can be refrigerated for up to 2 days.)*

● RASPBERRY GLAZE: Drain raspberries through sieve, pressing to remove seeds, and extract about 1-1/3 cups (325 mL) juice. In saucepan, whisk raspberry juice into cornstarch until smooth. Bring to boil over medium-high heat, stirring constantly; cook, stirring, for about 1 minute or until thickened and clear. Stir in sugar and lemon juice. Let cool.

● Line pan with 2-inch (5 cm) high waxed- or parchment-paper collar to prevent glaze from touching side of pan. Pour raspberry glaze evenly over cake. Refrigerate for at least 1-1/2 hours or until set. *(Cake can be refrigerated for up to 4 hours.)* Remove side of pan. Makes 12 servings.

TIPS

● You can substitute 1 cup (250 mL) extra-thick yogurt for plain; there is no need to drain it.

● Cracks may appear in the cheesecake if it is exposed to sudden temperature change or bakes in too hot an oven for too long. For the required steady oven temperature, resist opening the oven door during baking and don't neglect the water bath in the shallow pan. It ensures even, slow, moist cooking.

Apple Streusel Cheesecake ▼

2 cups	all-purpose flour	500 mL
1/2 cup	icing sugar	125 mL
1 tsp	ginger	5 mL
1 cup	cold butter, cubed	250 mL
	FILLING	
3	pkg (each 8 oz/250 g) cream cheese, softened	3
2/3 cup	granulated sugar	150 mL
1 cup	sour cream	250 mL
1 tsp	vanilla	5 mL
4	eggs	4
	TOPPING	
1/2 cup	packed brown sugar	125 mL
1/3 cup	rolled oats	75 mL
1/3 cup	all-purpose flour	75 mL
1/2 tsp	cinnamon	2 mL
1/4 cup	butter	50 mL
3	apples, peeled and cut into eighths	3

● In food processor, combine flour, icing sugar and ginger. Using on/off motion, cut in butter until pastry starts to come together in clumps. (Or in bowl, mix together flour, icing sugar and ginger; cut in butter until mixture resembles coarse crumbs; press into small handfuls until pastry holds together.)

● Press evenly into bottom and up side to top of 10-inch (3 L) springform pan. Refrigerate for 1 hour. Using fork, prick bottom all over. Bake in 350°F (180°C) oven for about 20 minutes or until golden brown. Let cool on rack.

● FILLING: In bowl, beat cream cheese with sugar until fluffy; beat in sour cream and vanilla. Beat in eggs, one at a time, beating until well combined; pour into cooled crust. Bake in 300°F (150°C) oven for about 45 minutes or until set around edge yet still jiggly in center. Transfer to rack.

● TOPPING: Meanwhile, in small bowl, mix together sugar, rolled oats, flour and cinnamon; with pastry blender or two knives, cut in three-quarters of the butter until mixture is crumbly. Set aside.

● In large skillet, melt remaining butter over medium-high heat; cook apples, turning once, for about 5 minutes or until golden brown and slightly softened.

● Arrange apples and any pan juices decoratively over cake. Sprinkle with rolled oats mixture; bake in 350°F (180°C) oven for 10 to 15 minutes or until topping is golden brown. Let cool on rack to room temperature. Refrigerate for at least 2 hours or until chilled. *(Cake can be refrigerated for up to 1 day.)* Makes 12 servings.

Quite simply, this is one of the finest cheesecakes ever tasted in the Test Kitchen.

Per serving: about
- 655 calories
- 46 g fat
- good source of iron
- 11 g protein
- 52 g carbohydrate

Chocolate Strawberry Mousse Cake ▶

Layers of bittersweet chocolate mousse and delicate pink strawberry mousse combine in a heavenly confection.

Per serving: about
- 520 calories
- 9 g protein
- 34 g fat
- 53 g carbohydrate
- good source of iron
- high source of fiber

1	8-1/2-inch (21 cm) Chocolate Sponge Cake (recipe follows)	1
2 cups	strawberries	500 mL
6 oz	bittersweet chocolate, coarsely chopped	175 g
2 cups	whipping cream	500 mL
2	egg whites	2
1 tbsp	granulated sugar	15 mL
	TOPPING	
1 cup	strawberries	250 mL
2 oz	bittersweet chocolate, melted	60 g

● Place 8-1/2-inch (2.25 L) springform pan without base on cake plate. Cut waxed paper into 10- x 3-inch (25 x 8 cm) strip; fit collar around inside of ring. Fit cake into pan. Slice 1 cup (250 mL) of the strawberries; arrange half over cake.

● In bowl over hot (not boiling) water, melt chocolate; let cool to room temperature, stirring occasionally.

● In large bowl, whip cream; set 2 cups (500 mL) aside for strawberry mousse. Fold half of the remaining cream into chocolate; fold in remaining cream.

● In separate bowl, beat egg whites until stiff but not dry peaks form; fold into chocolate mixture. Pour onto prepared cake, smoothing top. Arrange remaining sliced strawberries over top; refrigerate.

● In food processor or blender, purée remaining strawberries with sugar; fold into reserved whipped cream. Pour over strawberry layer, smoothing top. Cover lightly with plastic wrap and refrigerate until set, about 2 hours. *(Cake can be refrigerated for up to 24 hours.)*

● TOPPING: Remove plastic wrap, springform side and collar from cake. Dip strawberries into chocolate; arrange around top edge of cake. Serve immediately. Makes 10 servings.

CHOCOLATE SPONGE CAKE

3	eggs	3
1/2 cup	granulated sugar	125 mL
1/2 tsp	vanilla	2 mL
1/3 cup	all-purpose flour	75 mL
1/4 cup	unsweetened cocoa powder	50 mL
1/4 tsp	baking powder	1 mL
Pinch	salt	Pinch
3 tbsp	butter, melted	50 mL

● In bowl, beat eggs until foamy; gradually beat in sugar. Beat for 5 to 8 minutes or until batter falls in ribbons when beaters are lifted. Beat in vanilla.

● Stir together flour, cocoa powder, baking powder and salt; sift half over egg mixture and fold in. Fold in remaining flour mixture.

● Remove one-quarter of the batter to small bowl; gradually fold in butter. Gradually fold back into batter.

● Scrape into greased 8-1/2-inch (2.25 L) springform pan. Bake in 325°F (160°C) oven for 40 minutes or until cake springs back when lightly pressed. Let cool in pan for 20 minutes. Turn out onto rack; let cool completely. Makes 1 sponge cake.

Chocolate Strawberry Mousse Cake

Orange Espresso Cheesecake

1 cup	graham cracker crumbs	250 mL
3 tbsp	butter, melted	50 mL
2 tbsp	granulated sugar	25 mL
	FILLING	
4	pkg (each 8 oz/250 g) cream cheese, softened	4
1 cup	granulated sugar	250 mL
3 tbsp	all-purpose flour	50 mL
4	eggs	4
1 cup	sour cream	250 mL
2 tbsp	instant espresso powder or instant coffee granules	25 mL
2 tsp	grated orange rind	10 mL
1/4 cup	orange juice	50 mL
1/4 tsp	cinnamon	1 mL
	GARNISH	
2 tsp	grated orange rind	10 mL
4	chocolate-covered coffee beans (optional)	4

● Combine cracker crumbs, butter and sugar: press onto bottom of greased 10-inch (3 L) springform pan. Center pan on piece of foil; press foil to side of pan. Bake in 325°F (160°C) oven for 10 minutes. Let cool.

● FILLING: In large bowl, beat cream cheese with sugar; beat in flour. Beat in eggs, one at a time. Stir in sour cream. In separate bowl, stir together espresso powder, orange rind and juice and cinnamon; stir into cream cheese mixture. Pour over crust.

● Set pan in larger pan; pour in enough hot water to come 1 inch (2.5 cm) up sides. Bake in 325°F (160°C) oven for about 50 minutes or until top is set and no longer jiggly in center. Turn oven off. Quickly run knife around cake. Let stand in oven for 1 hour.

● Remove from larger pan and remove foil; let cool completely on rack. Cover and refrigerate for at least 8 hours or until thoroughly chilled. Let stand at room temperature for 1 hour before serving.

● GARNISH: Sprinkle orange rind over cake; arrange chocolate-covered coffee beans (if using) around edge. Makes 12 servings.

Espresso and orange deliver a sophisticated new flavor take to an ever-popular dessert classic.

Per serving: about
● 490 calories
● 10 g protein
● 37 g fat
● 31 g carbohydrate

Raspberry Lemon Dacquoise ▶

Created by pastry chef Marianne Sanders, this professional-style cake can be made ahead in stages. Prepare the cake layers, meringue and lemon syrup beforehand, then assemble a few hours before presentation.

Per serving: about
- 665 calories
- 43 g fat
- 10 g protein
- 64 g carbohydrate

1-1/2 cups	whipping cream	375 mL
2 cups	raspberries, blackberries or strawberries	500 mL
	LEMON SYRUP	
1/3 cup	granulated sugar	75 mL
1/3 cup	lemon juice	75 mL
	LEMON CURD	
1/3 cup	granulated sugar	75 mL
1 tsp	grated lemon rind	5 mL
1/4 cup	lemon juice	50 mL
1	egg	1
2 tbsp	butter	25 mL
	CAKE	
3/4 cup	butter, softened	175 mL
1-1/4 cups	granulated sugar	300 mL
3	eggs, separated	3
1 tsp	grated lemon rind	5 mL
2 cups	all-purpose flour	500 mL
2 tsp	baking powder	10 mL
3/4 cup	lukewarm milk	175 mL
	MERINGUE	
1 cup	almonds	250 mL
2 tbsp	cornstarch	25 mL
4	egg whites	4
2/3 cup	granulated sugar	150 mL
	BUTTERCREAM ICING	
4	egg whites	4
1 cup	granulated sugar	250 mL
1-1/3 cups	unsalted butter, softened	325 mL
	GARNISH	
1 cup	sliced almonds, toasted	250 mL

● LEMON SYRUP: In stainless steel saucepan, whisk sugar with lemon juice over medium heat until boiling and sugar is dissolved, about 1 minute. Let cool. *(Syrup can be refrigerated in airtight container for up to 1 week.)*

● LEMON CURD: In heavy stainless steel saucepan, whisk together sugar, lemon rind and juice, egg and butter; cook over medium-low heat, stirring constantly, for about 10 minutes or until thickened. Cover and refrigerate until chilled. *(Curd can be refrigerated in airtight container for up to 2 days.)*

● CAKE: Line base of 10-inch (3 L) springform pan with parchment or waxed paper; set aside. In bowl, beat butter with 1 cup (250 mL) of the sugar until light and fluffy. Beat in egg yolks until fluffy. Beat in lemon rind. Stir flour with baking powder; add to butter mixture alternately with milk, making three additions of flour mixture and two of milk.

● In separate bowl, beat egg whites until soft peaks form; gradually beat in remaining sugar until stiff peaks form Fold into batter. Spoon into prepared pan; bake in 350°F (180°C) oven for about 45 minutes or until golden and cake tester inserted in center comes out clean. Let cool in pan on rack. *(Cake can be wrapped in plastic wrap and stored for up to 2 days or frozen in rigid airtight container for up to 2 weeks.)*

● MERINGUE: Spread almonds on baking sheet; toast in 350°F (180°C) oven for 10 minutes or until golden. Meanwhile, cut two 10-inch (25 cm) circles of parchment or waxed paper; place on baking sheets.

● In food processor, finely grind almonds with cornstarch; set aside. In bowl, beat egg whites until soft peaks form; gradually beat in sugar until stiff peaks form. Working quickly, fold nut mixture into egg whites. Spread over prepared circles to within 1/4 inch (5 mm) of edge. Bake in 350°F (180°C) oven for 15 minutes or until golden. Turn oven off; let stand in oven for 10 minutes. Remove paper. *(Meringues can be loosely covered and stored at room temperature for up to 1 day.)*

● BUTTERCREAM ICING: In heatproof bowl, whisk egg whites with sugar. Heat over boiling water, whisking often, for 3 minutes

or until white and candy thermometer registers 110°F (43°C) or finger can remain in mixture for 10 seconds. Remove from heat. Using electric mixer, beat for 5 to 10 minutes or until very cool. Beat in butter, 2 tbsp (25 mL) at a time, beating until satiny. *(Icing can be refrigerated in airtight container for up to 1 week or frozen for up to 1 month; bring to room temperature before using and rewhip to lighten.)*

● ASSEMBLY: In bowl, whip cream; fold in lemon curd. Cut cake in half horizontally; place bottom layer on serving plate. Brush with half of the lemon syrup; spread with one-third of the whipped-cream mixture. Reserving a few raspberries for garnish, scatter one-third of the remaining raspberries over cream. Top with one of the meringue circles.

● Spread with another third of the whipped-cream mixture; scatter with another third of the raspberries. Top with remaining meringue; spread with remaining whipped cream and raspberries. Brush cut side of remaining cake layer with remaining lemon syrup. Invert onto raspberries.

● With sharp knife, trim any uneven edges of dacquoise, using scraps to fill any spaces between layers. Spread buttercream icing over top and side, smoothing with palette knife.

● GARNISH: Press almonds onto side of cake to cover. Garnish top with reserved berries. *(Dacquoise can be refrigerated for up to 24 hours; remove from refrigerator 30 minutes before serving.)* Makes 16 servings.

TIP: You can increase the meringue recipe by half and make three layers in order to have one left over to cut and use as garnish (as in the photo).

Peaches and Cream Meringue Cake

Celebrate summer with this combo of crunchy almond meringue, juicy fresh peaches and lightened whipped cream.

Per serving: about
- •185 calories
- • 11 g fat
- • 3 g protein
- • 20 g carbohydrate

TIP: If you don't have parchment paper, line baking sheet with foil. With blunt knife, make two circles on foil. Grease and flour circles.

1 cup	plain yogurt	250 mL
6	peaches or nectarines	6
1 cup	whipping cream	250 mL
1 tbsp	granulated sugar	15 mL
	Mint sprigs	
	MERINGUE	
1/4 cup	finely chopped blanched almonds	50 mL
2	egg whites	2
Pinch	each salt and cream of tartar	Pinch
1/2 cup	granulated sugar	125 mL
1/2 tsp	vanilla	2 mL
2 tsp	cornstarch	10 mL

● Pour yogurt into cheesecloth-lined sieve set over bowl; cover and refrigerate to drain for at least 3 hours or until reduced to 1/2 cup (125 mL). Discard liquid.

● Meanwhile, line baking sheet with parchment paper. Using 8-inch (1.2 L) round cake pan as guide, draw two circles; turn paper over. Set aside.

● MERINGUE: Spread almonds in cake pan; bake in 350°F (180°C) oven for 6 minutes or until light golden. Let cool completely.

● In bowl, beat together egg whites, salt and cream of tartar until soft peaks form; gradually beat in sugar until stiff glossy peaks form. Stir in vanilla. Fold in cornstarch and almonds.

● Spoon onto each circle, spreading evenly to edges. Bake in 275°F (140°C) oven for 1-1/2 hours or until tops are firm to the touch and undersides are dry. Transfer to rack; let cool completely. Peel off paper. *(Meringues can be wrapped in foil and stored in cool dry place for up to 3 days.)*

● Peel and slice peaches; set aside. In bowl, whip cream; beat in sugar. Fold in drained yogurt.

● Place one of the meringues on serving plate; spread with half of the cream mixture. Top with two-thirds of the peaches. Top with remaining meringue; spread with remaining cream mixture. Garnish top with remaining peaches. Refrigerate for about 30 minutes or until meringues soften slightly. Garnish with mint sprigs. Makes 10 servings.

Cranberry Yogurt Kuchen

1-1/2 cups	all-purpose flour	375 mL
1/2 cup	granulated sugar	125 mL
1/3 cup	butter, melted	75 mL
1-1/2 tsp	baking powder	7 mL
2	egg whites	2
1 tsp	vanilla	5 mL
2 cups	cranberries (fresh or frozen)	500 mL
	TOPPING	
2 cups	1% or 2% plain yogurt	500 mL
1	egg	1
3/4 cup	granulated sugar	175 mL
2 tbsp	all-purpose flour	25 mL
2 tsp	grated lemon or orange rind	10 mL
1 tsp	vanilla	5 mL
2 tsp	icing sugar	10 mL

● In food processor or bowl, combine flour, sugar, butter, baking powder, egg whites and vanilla, mixing well. Press over base of lightly greased 10-inch (3 L) springform pan; sprinkle evenly with cranberries.

● TOPPING: In bowl, whisk together yogurt, egg, sugar, flour, lemon rind and vanilla until smooth; pour over cranberries. Bake in 350°F (180°C) oven for 60 to 70 minutes or until crust is golden. Sift icing sugar over top just before serving warm or cold. Makes 12 servings.

This updated version of a traditional kuchen has a baking powder-raised base. Other fruit, especially partridgeberries, can replace the cranberries that peek through the creamy topping.

Per serving: about
- 235 calories
- 6 g fat
- 5 g protein
- 39 g carbohydrate

Rhubarb Custard Torte

3/4 cup	butter	175 mL
1/3 cup	granulated sugar	75 mL
2	egg yolks	2
2 cups	all-purpose flour	500 mL
1 tsp	baking powder	5 mL
1/2 tsp	salt	2 mL
	FILLING	
6 cups	chopped rhubarb (1-inch/2.5 cm pieces)	1.5 L
1/2 cup	granulated sugar	125 mL
1/4 cup	quick-cooking tapioca	50 mL
1/2 tsp	cinnamon	2 mL
6	eggs	6
2 cups	sour cream	500 mL
1/2 cup	packed brown sugar	125 mL
2 tsp	finely grated lemon rind	10 mL
1 tsp	vanilla	5 mL
	Icing sugar	
	Grated lemon rind	

● In large bowl, beat butter with sugar; beat in egg yolks until light and fluffy. Combine flour, baking powder and salt; add to egg mixture, mixing with hands until crumbly.

Press two-thirds of the mixture onto bottom of 10-inch (3 L) springform pan. Bake in 400°F (200°C) oven for 10 minutes or just until light golden. Let cool. Press remaining mixture up side of pan.

● FILLING: In heavy stainless steel saucepan, stir together rhubarb, granulated sugar, tapioca and cinnamon; let stand for 15 minutes. Stir in 1/4 cup (50 mL) water; bring to boil. Reduce heat to medium-low; cover and cook, stirring often, for about 10 minutes or just until rhubarb is tender but not mushy. *(Mixture should be quite thick.)* Let cool slightly; pour over crust.

● In large bowl, whisk eggs for about 2 minutes or until frothy; stir in sour cream, brown sugar, lemon rind and vanilla. Pour over rhubarb; bake in 350°F (180°C) oven for about 1 hour or until top is golden and custard is set. Let cool on rack. Cover and refrigerate for at least 3 hours or until chilled. *(Torte can be refrigerated for up to 12 hours.)* Run knife around crust; remove side of pan. Sprinkle icing sugar over top, then lemon rind in center. Makes 8 servings.

Spring's first fruit stars in a refreshing dessert with a tender shortcake crust and a juicy filling.

Per serving: about
- 595 calories
- 31 g fat
- good source of calcium
- 11 g protein
- 70 g carbohydrate
- good source of iron

TIP: If you use frozen rhubarb, place it in a large sieve and pour hot water over it for a few seconds before proceeding with the recipe. Increase the tapioca to 1/3 cup (75 mL).

Lemon-Glazed Pound Cake ▼

Lemon adds a tingle to this dense, moist pound cake, made into a very special-occasion dessert by a medley of berries and orange slices in a glistening caramel sauce.

Per serving: about
- 435 calories
- 6 g protein
- 11 g fat
- 79 g carbohydrate
- good source of iron

Orange Caramel Sauce
(recipe follows)

POUND CAKE

1-1/2 cups	light sour cream	375 mL
1 tsp	baking soda	5 mL
2/3 cup	butter, softened	150 mL
2-2/3 cups	granulated sugar	650 mL
5	eggs	5
1-1/2 tsp	vanilla	7 mL
4-1/2 cups	sifted cake-and-pastry flour	1.125 L
1 tbsp	grated lemon rind	15 mL
1/4 tsp	salt	1 mL

GLAZE

3/4 cup	icing sugar	175 mL
2 tsp	grated lemon rind	10 mL
2 tbsp	lemon juice	25 mL

● POUND CAKE: Stir sour cream with baking soda; set aside. In large bowl, beat butter until fluffy; gradually beat in sugar until well combined. Beat in eggs, one at a time, scraping down bowl and beating well after each addition. Stir in vanilla.

● Stir together flour, lemon rind and salt; stir into batter alternately with sour cream mixture, making three additions of flour mixture and two of sour cream.

● Scrape into well-greased 10-inch (4 L) tube pan. Bake in 325°F (160°C) oven for about 1 hour and 30 minutes or until cake tester comes out clean. Let cool in pan for 30 minutes. Turn out onto serving plate; let cool completely.

● GLAZE: In small bowl, whisk together icing sugar, lemon rind and juice; pour over cake, spreading evenly over top and letting excess drip down sides. *(Cake can be covered and stored for up to 1 day.)* Serve with Orange Caramel Sauce. Makes 16 servings.

ORANGE CARAMEL SAUCE

1-1/3 cups	strained fresh orange juice	325 mL
1 cup	granulated sugar	250 mL

● In small saucepan, heat orange juice just until warm; keep warm.

● In heavy saucepan, stir sugar with 1/3 cup (75 mL) water over medium heat until dissolved, brushing down side of pan if necessary with pastry brush dipped in water. Increase heat to medium-high; boil, without stirring, until pale caramel color.

● Stirring constantly, gradually pour in orange juice; boil for 5 minutes or until reduced to 1-1/4 cups (300 mL). Cover and refrigerate for at least 6 hours or until thickened. Makes 1-1/4 cups (300 mL).

Per tbsp (15 mL): about
- 50 calories
- trace protein
- 0 g fat
- 12 g carbohydrate

Pumpkin Chiffon Spice Cake

7	eggs, separated	7
1-1/4 cups	granulated sugar	300 mL
3/4 cup	canned pumpkin purée	175 mL
1/2 cup	vegetable oil	125 mL
1/2 cup	water	125 mL
1-3/4 cups	all-purpose flour	425 mL
1/4 cup	cornstarch	50 mL
1 tbsp	baking powder	15 mL
1-1/2 tsp	cinnamon	7 mL
1/2 tsp	each ground cloves and grated nutmeg	2 mL
1/4 tsp	salt	1 mL
1/4 cup	finely chopped candied ginger (optional)	50 mL

● In large bowl, beat egg yolks with 1 cup (250 mL) of the sugar for about 3 minutes or until pale and thickened. Beat in pumpkin, oil and water. Stir together flour, cornstarch, baking powder, cinnamon, cloves, nutmeg and salt; sift one-third over pumpkin mixture and gently fold in until no lumps remain. Fold in remaining flour mixture in two additions.

● In separate bowl, beat egg whites until soft peaks form; gradually beat in remaining sugar until stiff peaks form. Fold one-third into pumpkin mixture; fold in candied ginger (if using). Fold in remaining whites.

● Scrape into ungreased 10-inch (4 L) tube pan; bake in 350°F (180°C) oven for 50 to 55 minutes or until firm and golden. Invert onto pan's legs; let cake hang until cool. Remove from pan. Makes 12 servings.

A *chiffon cake is slightly less decadent than most cakes but still impressively delicious. Serve with a scoop of low-fat frozen yogurt, if desired.*

Per serving: about
- 290 calories
- 12 g fat
- 6 g protein
- 39 g carbohydrate

Double Apple Cake

2	apples	2
2/3 cup	packed brown sugar	150 mL
1/4 cup	butter, softened	50 mL
1	egg	1
1/4 cup	low-fat plain yogurt	50 mL
1 tsp	vanilla	5 mL
1-2/3 cups	sifted cake-and-pastry flour	400 mL
1-1/2 tsp	ginger	7 mL
1-1/2 tsp	baking powder	7 mL
1/2 tsp	baking soda	2 mL
Pinch	salt	Pinch
2/3 cup	The Best Applesauce (recipe, p. 35)	150 mL
	TOPPING	
3 tbsp	packed brown sugar	50 mL
2 tsp	water	10 mL
1/2 tsp	cinnamon	2 mL

● Peel, core and thinly slice apples; set aside.

● In bowl, beat sugar with butter until crumbly; beat in egg. Beat in yogurt and vanilla. Combine flour, ginger, baking powder, baking soda and salt; fold into butter mixture alternately with applesauce, making three additions of flour mixture and two of applesauce. Spoon into lightly greased 9-inch (2.5 L) springform pan. Arrange apples in overlapping concentric circles on top.

● TOPPING: Combine sugar, water and cinnamon; brush over apples. Bake in 350°F (180°C) oven for 40 minutes or until cake tester inserted in center comes out clean. Let cool in pan on rack for 5 minutes. Remove side of pan; let cool completely. Makes 10 servings.

T *hanks to applesauce and yogurt in the batter, you can bake up a tender, moist cake without a lot of butter or oil.*

Per serving: about
- 220 calories
- 6 g fat
- 3 g protein
- 40 g carbohydrate

Holiday Apple Cake

*For fruitcake lovers
everywhere — a citrussy
apple-and-dried-cranberry
version that packs in lots of
fruity flavor without any of
the usual sticky sweetness.
Even if you're not a fan of
fruitcake, this one may make
you change your mind!*

Per each of 20 servings: about
• 340 calories   • 4 g protein
• 14 g fat   • 50 g carbohydrate

1 cup	currants	250 mL
1/4 cup	rye whisky	50 mL
3 cups	all-purpose flour	750 mL
2 tsp	cinnamon	10 mL
1 tsp	each baking soda and grated nutmeg	5 mL
1/4 tsp	each salt and ground cloves	1 mL
1-1/4 cups	packed brown sugar	300 mL
3/4 cup	vegetable oil	175 mL
1/2 cup	orange juice	125 mL
3	eggs	3
1 tbsp	each grated orange and lemon rind	15 mL
2-1/2 cups	thinly sliced peeled apples	625 mL
1 cup	chopped toasted hazelnuts, unblanched almonds or pecans	250 mL
1/2 cup	dried cranberries or raisins	125 mL
	LEMON WHISKY GLAZE	
1 cup	granulated sugar	250 mL
1/4 cup	lemon juice	50 mL
1/4 cup	rye whisky	50 mL

● In small bowl, combine currants with whisky; set aside.

● In large bowl, combine flour, cinnamon, baking soda, nutmeg, salt and cloves.

● In separate bowl, beat together sugar, oil and orange juice; beat in eggs and orange and lemon rinds. Pour over dry ingredients; stir until combined. Stir in currant mixture, apples, nuts and cranberries.

● Spoon into greased 10-inch (3 L) Bundt pan. Bake in 350°F (180°C) oven for about 1 hour or until golden brown and cake tester inserted in center comes out clean. Let cool completely in pan on rack.

● LEMON WHISKY GLAZE: In saucepan, stir sugar with lemon juice. Bring to boil over medium-high heat; boil for 1 minute. Stir in whisky. Pour half over cooled cake.

● Remove cake from pan; invert onto serving plate. Drizzle with remaining glaze. Let stand, covered, for 1 day. *(Cake can be wrapped in plastic wrap and frozen in rigid airtight container for up to 1 month.)* Makes 18 to 20 servings.

TIP: To toast hazelnuts, bake whole nuts on baking sheet in 350°F (180°C) oven for 8 to 10 minutes or until fragrant. Place on clean tea towel; rub vigorously to remove most of the skins.

APPLES FOR BAKING AND COOKING

Here's a handy guide to help you pick the right apple for cooking or baking.

● **For slaws and salads,** use Cortland apples because they don't discolor quickly.

● **For cakes and sauces,** choose apples that hold their shape well: Cortland, Golden Delicious, Idared, Jonagold, Mutsu (Crispin), Northern Spy and Spartan.

● **For puréed sauces and spreads,** choose apples that break down easily: Empire, Gravenstein, McIntosh, Royal Gala, Granny Smith and Transparent.

● **For pies and baked apples,** use apples that hold their shape well and deliver the best flavor: Golden Delicious, Idared, Mutsu (Crispin) and Northern Spy.

Rhubarb Coffee Cake

1/2 cup	butter, softened	125 mL
1 cup	packed brown sugar	250 mL
2	eggs	2
1 cup	buttermilk	250 mL
1 tsp	vanilla	5 mL
1-1/3 cups	all-purpose flour	325 mL
1 cup	whole wheat flour	250 mL
2 tsp	baking powder	10 mL
1/2 tsp	each baking soda and cinnamon	2 mL
1/4 tsp	salt	1 mL
3 cups	chopped rhubarb	750 mL
	TOPPING	
1/2 cup	sliced almonds	125 mL
1/3 cup	packed brown sugar	75 mL
1/2 tsp	cinnamon	2 mL

● TOPPING: In small bowl, combine almonds, sugar and cinnamon; set aside.

● In large bowl, beat butter with brown sugar until fluffy; beat in eggs, one at a time, beating well after each addition. Beat in buttermilk and vanilla. Stir together all-purpose flour, whole wheat flour, baking powder, baking soda, cinnamon and salt; stir into butter mixture just until blended.

● Spread into greased 13- x 9-inch (3.5 L) cake pan. Sprinkle rhubarb over batter; sprinkle with topping. Bake in 350°F (180°C) oven for about 1 hour or until cake tester inserted in center comes out clean. Let cool in pan on rack. Makes 12 servings.

H*omey — but never homely — this buttermilk cake basks under a topping of pink rhubarb and crunchy almonds.*

Per serving: about
- 300 calories
- 6 g protein
- 11 g fat
- 45 g carbohydrate

Berry Coconut Cake

1/2 cup	butter, softened	125 mL
3/4 cup	granulated sugar	175 mL
2	eggs	2
1 tsp	vanilla	5 mL
1-1/2 cups	all purpose flour	375 mL
1-1/2 tsp	baking powder	7 mL
1 tsp	baking sodar	5 mL
1/4 tsp	salt	1 mL
1 cup	sour cream	250 mL
3/4 cup	each raspberries and blueberries	175 mL
	TOPPING	
1 cup	shredded coconut	250 mL
1/2 cup	packed brown sugar	125 mL
2 tbsp	butter, softened	25 mL
1 tbsp	all-purpose flour	15 mL
1/4 tsp	cinnamon	1 mL

● TOPPING; In small bowl, combine coconut, sugar, butter, flour and cinnamon; set aside.

● In large bowl, beat butter with sugar until fluffy. Beat in eggs, one at a time, beating well after each addition. Beat in vanilla. Stir together flour, baking powder, baking soda and salt; stir half into butter mixture. Stir in sour cream. Stir in remaining flour mixture.

● Spread in greased 9-inch (2.5 L) square cake pan. Sprinkle with raspberries and blueberries. Sprinkle with topping. Bake in 325°F (160°C) oven for 60 to 75 minutes or until cake tester inserted in center comes out clean. Let cool in pan on rack. Makes 9 servings.

W*hen you need a quick and easy cake for a potluck dinner, as a gift for the cottage hostess or to serve for brunch, this moist, berry-flavored one fits the bill deliciously.*

Per serving: about
- 425 calories
- 5 g protein
- 21 g fat
- 54 g carbohydrate

Gowrie House Blueberry Coffee Cake

Bursting with wild blueberries, this lemon-crusted cinnamony cake is traditionally served at breakfast, but is just as delicious for dessert or teatime.

Per serving: about
- 390 calories
- 6 g protein
- 10 g fat
- 72 g carbohydrate

1/2 cup	butter, softened	125 mL
2 cups	granulated sugar (approx)	500 mL
2	eggs	2
3-1/2 cups	all-purpose flour	875 mL
1 tsp	baking soda	5 mL
1 tsp	salt	5 mL
1 tsp	grated lemon rind	5 mL
1 cup	milk	250 mL
3 cups	blueberries (fresh or frozen)	750 mL
1 tbsp	cinnamon	15 mL
	TOPPING	
1/4 cup	granulated sugar	50 mL
1/4 cup	lemon juice	50 mL

● In large bowl, beat butter with sugar until fluffy. Beat in eggs, one at a time, beating well after each addition. Stir together flour, baking soda, salt and lemon rind; add to butter mixture alternately with milk, making three additions of dry and two of milk. Fold in blueberries.

● Scrape into greased 13- x 9-inch (3.5 L) cake pan. Sprinkle with cinnamon and 1 tbsp (15 mL) more sugar. Bake in 350°F (180°C) oven for 1 hour or until cake tester inserted in center comes out clean.

● TOPPING: In small saucepan, dissolve sugar in 1/4 cup (50 mL) water over medium heat; cook for 4 minutes. Stir in lemon juice. Prick holes in top of cake; brush lemon syrup over cake. Serve warm. Makes 12 servings.

Tunnel-of-Cranberry Coffee Cake

What fun to cut into a golden, buttery bundt cake like this one and discover a ruby-red jewel of a filling — yours to savor with every bite.

Per serving: about
- 345 calories
- 5 g protein
- 15 g fat
- 48 g carbohydrate

1/2 cup	chopped pecans or almonds	125 mL
1-1/2 cups	cranberries (fresh or frozen)	375 mL
1/2 cup	packed brown sugar	125 mL
1/4 tsp	grated nutmeg	1 mL
1 tbsp	icing sugar	15 mL
	CAKE	
3/4 cup	butter, softened	175 mL
1-1/2 cups	packed brown sugar	375 mL
3	eggs	3
2 tsp	vanilla	10 mL
3 cups	all-purpose flour	750 mL
1-1/2 tsp	baking powder	7 mL
1/2 tsp	each baking soda and salt	2 mL
1-1/2 cups	sour cream	375 mL

● Sprinkle nuts in bottom of greased 10-inch (3 L) Bundt pan; set aside.

● In saucepan, bring cranberries, brown sugar, 1/4 cup (50 mL) water and nutmeg to boil; reduce heat and simmer, stirring often,

for about 7 minutes or until very thick and spoon scraped across bottom of pan leaves strip that fills in slowly. Let cool completely.

● CAKE: In bowl, beat butter with sugar until fluffy; beat in eggs, one at a time, beating well after each addition. Beat in vanilla. Stir together flour, baking powder, baking soda and salt; stir into butter mixture alternately with sour cream, making three additions of flour mixture and two of sour cream.

● Spoon half of the batter into prepared pan, smoothing top. Drop cranberry mixture by spoonfuls in ring around center of batter, leaving 3/4-inch (2 cm) border on both sides. Spoon remaining batter on top, smoothing gently.

● Bake in 350°F (180°C) oven for 60 to 75 minutes or until cake tester inserted in center of cake comes out clean. Let cool in pan on rack for 10 minutes; invert onto rack and let cool completely. Transfer to serving plate; dust with icing sugar. Makes 16 servings.

Banana Split Roll ▼

1/3 cup	butter, softened	75 mL
3/4 cup	granulated sugar	175 mL
3	egg yolks	3
2/3 cup	mashed bananas	150 mL
1/2 cup	buttermilk	125 mL
1 cup	all-purpose flour	250 mL
3/4 tsp	baking powder	4 mL
3/4 tsp	baking soda	4 mL
1/2 tsp	salt	2 mL
6	egg whites	6
	FILLING AND GARNISH	
1 cup	whipping cream	250 mL
2 tbsp	icing sugar	25 mL
1 tsp	vanilla	5 mL
	Strawberry sauce	
	Banana slices	
	Pineapple pieces	
	Chocolate sauce	

● Grease 17-1/2- x 11-1/2-inch (45 x 29 cm) jelly roll pan. Line with waxed paper; grease and flour paper. Set aside.

● In large bowl, beat butter with sugar until light and fluffy. Beat in egg yolks, one at a time, beating well after each addition. Mix in bananas and buttermilk. Stir together flour, baking powder, baking soda and salt; add to batter all at once, stirring just until combined.

● In separate bowl, beat egg whites until soft peaks form. Stir about one-quarter into batter; fold in remaining egg whites.

● Spoon into prepared pan, smoothing top. Bake in 350°F (180°C) oven for about 20 minutes or until golden. Loosen edges with knife; let cool in pan on rack for 5 minutes. Invert onto clean tea towel; peel off paper. Starting at long side, roll up cake in towel. Let cool completely on rack.

● FILLING AND GARNISH: In bowl, whip cream; beat in sugar and vanilla. Unroll cake and spread with cream mixture; roll up gently. *(Roll can be covered and refrigerated for up to 8 hours.)*

● To serve, pool strawberry sauce on each dessert plate. Top with 3 thin slices or 1 thick slice banana roll; garnish with banana and pineapple. Drizzle with chocolate sauce. Makes 12 servings.

Enjoy all the flavors of a banana split — ripe bananas, pineapple, chocolate and strawberry — in an eye-appealing rolled cake.

Per serving: about
- 445 calories
- 17 g fat
- 6 g protein
- 71 g carbohydrate

Fruit on its Own

Fruit goes solo in this seasonal collection of compotes, stews, purées and summer-fresh salads. Don't let the ease of preparation fool you, though — there's a wallop of intense fruit flavor in each delicious spoonful!

Peach and Plum Compote

Fresh mint highlights a bowl of sweet yet tart poached peaches and plums.

Per serving: about
- 120 calories
- 1 g protein
- 1 g fat
- 1 g protein
- 29 g carbohydrate

TIP: For a nonalcoholic version, substitute white grape juice or apple juice for the wine, and increase sugar to 1/2 cup (125 mL).

5	peaches or nectarines	5
1/2 cup	Riesling or other fruity white wine	125 mL
1/3 cup	packed brown sugar or granulated sugar	75 mL
1	strip lemon rind	1
1	stick cinnamon	1
6	plums	6
2 tsp	chopped fresh mint (or 3/4 tsp/4 mL dried)	10 mL
	Fresh mint sprigs	

● Peel peaches; cut into 1/2-inch (1 cm) thick slices. In large shallow saucepan, combine wine, sugar, lemon rind, cinnamon stick and 1/2 cup (125 mL) water; bring to boil. Add peaches and return to boil; reduce heat to medium and simmer, stirring occasionally, for 8 minutes.

● Meanwhile, cut plums into 1/2-inch (1 cm) thick slices. Add to saucepan; simmer, stirring occasionally, for about 7 minutes or until fruit is tender and liquid is slightly thickened. Discard lemon rind and cinnamon.

● Stir in chopped mint. Serve warm or chilled garnished with mint sprigs. *(Compote can be refrigerated in airtight container for up to 1 day.)* Makes 6 servings.

PERFECT PEACHES AND NECTARINES
Canadian peaches and nectarines are available from mid-July through late September.

● Early peach varieties are best enjoyed right away. By mid-August, freestone preserving peaches are available. They can also be enjoyed fresh but are perfect for making jams and chutneys, or for canning and freezing. Nectarines are in season beginning mid-August.
● When buying peaches, look for fruit that's relatively firm, with a smooth skin, sweet aroma and clear, creamy yellow background color. The pink blush on a peach tells its variety, not its ripeness. Nectarines should have bright-red coloring over a yellow background. Don't choose fruit with wrinkled skin or a greenish tinge because it'll never sweeten. Avoid excessively soft, bruised or blemished fruit; choose fruit that yields gently to the touch.
● Peaches and nectarines are picked when mature but firm for the journey to market and most will need a little extra ripening at home. Keep them at room temperature out of direct sun until ripening begins and the skin yields slightly to gentle pressure. (Sealing them in a paper bag can hasten the process.) Ripe fruit should be stored in a single layer in the refrigerator for up to 5 days.
● Use overripe peaches and nectarines at once in recipes where their appearance isn't important.

Apricot Compote ▲

Dried apricots have an intensely perfumed flavor that translates well into a compote, here dressed up with raisins, cinnamon and orange.

Per serving: about
- 145 calories
- trace fat
- good source of iron
- 2 g protein
- 36 g carbohydrate
- high source of fiber

2 cups	dried apricots (about 11 oz/312 g)	500 mL
1/4 cup	raisins	50 mL
2	sticks cinnamon, broken in half	2
4	strips (6 inch/15 cm long) orange rind	4
1 cup	orange juice	250 mL

● In saucepan, combine apricots, raisins, cinnamon sticks, orange rind and juice and 2-1/2 cups (625 mL) water; bring to boil. Cover, reduce heat and simmer for 20 minutes or until apricots are tender. Discard cinnamon sticks; let cool. Serve at room temperature or chilled. *(Compote can be refrigerated in airtight container for up to 12 hours.)* Makes 6 servings.

TIP: Use a paring knife or channel knife to cut 6-inch (15 cm) strips of rind off a firm, washed orange.

Rhubarb Compote

1 cup	granulated sugar	250 mL
1/2 cup	water	125 mL
1	Stick (1/2-inch/1 cm) cinnamon	1
6 cups	chopped rhubarb (1-inch/2.5 cm pieces)	1.5 L

● In top of double boiler, combine sugar, water and cinnamon stick; bring to boil over direct heat.

● Place over gently boiling water; add rhubarb. Cover and cook for 15 minutes; turn off heat. Let cool in pan over water, without stirring. Discard cinnamon stick. Makes 3-1/2 cups (875 mL).

The secret to keeping rhubarb chunks whole is this gentle poaching and no stirring.

Per 1/2 cup (125 mL): about
• 135 calories • 1 g protein
• trace fat • 33 g carbohydrate

Clementines in Orange Syrup

8	firm clementines	8
1-1/2 cups	orange juice	375 mL
1-1/4 cups	granulated sugar	300 mL
1/3 cup	lemon juice	75 mL

● In large saucepan, combine unpeeled clementines and 8 cups (2 L) cold water; cover and bring to boil over medium-high heat. Boil for 45 seconds. Drain and transfer to bowl of ice and cold water; let soak for about 15 minutes or until chilled and firm. Drain and cut horizontally into 1/4-inch (5 mm) thick slices, discarding ends.

● In saucepan, bring orange juice, sugar and lemon juice to boil over medium heat. Add clementines; simmer gently for about 25 minutes or until rind is tender and pulp is very soft but not falling apart. *(Clementines and syrup can be prepared to this point and refrigerated in separate airtight containers for up to 24 hours.)*

● With slotted spoon, gently transfer clementines to serving dish; set aside. Boil syrup over medium heat, stirring occasionally, for 10 to 15 minutes or until thickened. Pour over clementines. Serve at room temperature or cool. Makes 4 servings.

This refreshing dessert is equally delicious with mandarins.

Per serving: about
• 425 calories • 3 g protein
• 1 g fat • 108 g carbohydrate
• very high source of fiber

The Best Applesauce

3 lb	apples (about 14)	1.5 kg
1/4 tsp	cinnamon (optional)	1 mL
2 tbsp	granulated sugar (optional)	25 mL

● Peel, core and slice apples. In saucepan, bring apples, 1/2 cup (125 mL) water and cinnamon (if using) to boil; cover, reduce heat and simmer, stirring occasionally, for 20 minutes or until tender. (Or in microwaveable dish, microwave, uncovered, at High for 12 minutes, stirring twice; let stand for 5 minutes.)

● Purée in food processor or push through food mill (or mash with potato masher for chunkier version). Sweeten with sugar (if using) while still warm. Makes 4 cups (1 L).

Why buy — when home-made tastes better, freezes into convenient portions for quick desserts and is so easy to make on the stove top or in the microwave oven!

Per 1/2 cup (125 mL): about
• 80 calories • trace protein
• trace fat • 20 g carbohydrate

Compote Keeper

If compote is something your family really enjoys, why not make it in a four-batch amount? Or do up the whole amount and have enough for gifts. Pack the dried fruit in jars and tie on a fancy ribbon, with instructions for simmering.

Per serving: about
- 240 calories
- trace fat
- good source of iron
- 2 g protein
- 64 g carbohydrate
- very high source of fiber

6 cups	dried apple slices (12 oz/375 g)	1.5 L
4 cups	dried apricots (1-1/2 lb/750 g)	1 L
2 cups	dried pitted prunes (12 oz/375 g)	500 mL
2 cups	dried pear halves (8 oz/250 g)	500 mL
1-1/2 cups	raisins (8 oz/250 g)	375 mL
1/2 cup	dried pitted cherries (3 oz/75 g)	125 mL
8	whole cloves	8
4	sticks cinnamon	4

● In large bowl, toss together apples, apricots, prunes, pears, raisins and cherries. Divide among 4 gift bags or jars. Divide cloves and cinnamon among bags; seal. Makes 16 cups (4 L).

TO MAKE COMPOTE
● In saucepan, combine 4 cups (1 L) water, 1/4 cup (50 mL) granulated sugar and 4 slices orange or lemon. Add 4 cups (1 L) Compote Keeper; bring to boil. Cover, reduce heat and simmer for 15 minutes or until fruit is tender. With slotted spoon, transfer fruit to serving bowl.

● Boil liquid for 1 minute or until thickened slightly; pour over fruit. *(Compote can be refrigerated for up to 1 week; to serve, add up to 1/2 cup/125 mL boiling water if desired.)* Makes 6 servings.

Red and Black Fruit Salad

Luscious watermelon adds an unexpected crispness to a summer berry medley. For an all-red fruit version, replace blackberries with more raspberries.

Per serving: about
- 135 calories
- 1 g fat
- high source of fiber
- 1 g protein
- 33 g carbohydrate

6	red plums	6
1 cup	bottled red fruit nectar	250 mL
	Rind of 1 orange, cut in strips	
1/4 cup	granulated sugar	50 mL
1 cup	blackberries	250 mL
2 cups	raspberries	500 mL
1 cup	cubed seeded watermelon	250 mL

● Halve and pit plums; quarter if large. Place, cut side down, in single layer in shallow microwaveable dish; pierce skins in several places.

● Add fruit nectar and orange rind; sprinkle with sugar. Cover and microwave at Medium (50% power) for 5 minutes or until tender-firm, rotating dish halfway through. Do not overcook.

● Add blackberries; cover and let stand until completely cool. Discard orange rind. Gently mix in raspberries and watermelon. Cover and refrigerate until chilled. Makes 6 servings.

Cantaloupe and Berry Combo

2 cups	sliced strawberries	500 mL
2 tbsp	granulated sugar	25 mL
2 tbsp	kirsch (optional)	25 mL
1 tbsp	lemon juice	15 mL
1	cantaloupe	1
1 cup	blueberries	250 mL

● In blender or food processor, purée strawberries. Add sugar, kirsch (if using) and lemon juice; mix until combined.

● Peel and halve cantaloupe; scoop out seeds and cut into bite-size pieces. Divide cantaloupe and blueberries among stemmed glasses; drizzle with strawberry sauce. Makes 4 servings.

TIP: For an eye-catching presentation, garnish each serving with a strawberry fan — just slice strawberry from tip almost through to top, then fan out slices.

Anne Lindsay came up with the ultimate summer-fruit combo and the extra-easy, fragrantly sweet sauce. A one-bowlful serving is a powerhouse of vitamin C and beta-carotene.

Per serving: about
- 115 calories
- 1 g fat
- 2 g protein
- 28 g carbohydrate

Ginger Citrus Fruit Salad ▼

2	grapefruit	2
4	oranges	4
2	kiwifruits	2
2 tbsp	finely chopped preserved or crystallized ginger	25 mL

● Cut slice from top and bottom of each grapefruit and orange; cut off skin, removing outside membrane. Working over bowl to catch juices, cut away sections from inner membranes.

● Peel kiwifruits and cut in half lengthwise; cut into slices crosswise.

● In serving bowl, combine grapefruit, oranges, juices, kiwifruits and ginger (if using preserved ginger, stir in 1 tbsp/15 mL syrup). Cover and let stand for 1 hour before serving. *(Salad can be covered and refrigerated for up to 8 hours; bring to room temperature before serving.)* Makes 4 servings.

Here's Anne Lindsay's healthy winter fruit salad. Garnish with slices of star fruit.

Per serving: about
- 150 calories
- 1 g fat
- high source of fiber
- 2 g protein
- 37 g carbohydrate

Spoon Desserts

The Italians call these desserts *dolci da cucchiaio* — velvety-smooth mousses, custards, puddings, ices and other frozen confections that slip down ever so easily and seductively. Here's a luscious selection to tempt you.

Mandarin Praline Trifle ◀

3	cans (each 10 oz/284 mL) mandarin oranges	3
2/3 cup	orange marmalade	150 mL
1/4 cup	amaretto liqueur	50 mL
1-1/2 cups	whipping cream	375 mL
	CUSTARD	
5	egg yolks	5
2-1/2 cups	milk	625 mL
1/2 cup	granulated sugar	125 mL
1/3 cup	cornstarch	75 mL
	CAKE	
6	eggs, separated	6
1-1/4 cups	granulated sugar	300 mL
1-1/2 tsp	vanilla	7 mL
Pinch	salt	Pinch
3/4 cup	all-purpose flour	175 mL
	PRALINE	
3/4 cup	sliced almonds, toasted	175 mL
1 cup	granulated sugar	250 mL

● CUSTARD: In bowl, whisk together egg yolks, 1/2 cup (125 mL) of the milk, sugar and cornstarch. In saucepan, heat remaining milk over medium heat until bubbles form around edge; gradually whisk into yolk mixture. Return to pan; cook, whisking, for 5 minutes or until thickened. Pour into bowl; place plastic wrap directly on surface. Refrigerate for 4 hours or until cool. *(Custard can be refrigerated for up to 2 days.)*

● CAKE: In bowl, beat egg yolks with 1/2 cup (125 mL) of the sugar until thickened; stir in vanilla. In second bowl, beat egg whites with salt until soft peaks form; gradually beat in remaining sugar until stiff peaks form. Alternately fold into egg yolk mixture along with flour, making three additions of egg whites and two of flour. Spread in two greased waxed paper-lined 13- x 9-inch (3.5 L) cake pans. Bake in 375°F (190°C) oven for 15 to 20 minutes or until top springs back.

● PRALINE: Meanwhile, arrange almonds in 9- x 7-inch (23 x 18 cm) rectangle on greased baking sheet. In heavy saucepan, dissolve sugar in 1/3 cup (75 mL) water over medium-high heat; boil, without stirring, for 5 to 8 minutes or until caramel color. Pour over almonds; let cool. Break one-third into 5 pieces; set aside. Finely chop remaining praline in food processor. *(Pralines can be stored in separate airtight containers for up to 5 days.)*

● Drain oranges; reserve 5 sections. Press marmalade through sieve to make 1/2 cup (125 mL). Invert cakes onto cutting board; turn over. Cut into quarters through paper to make layers. Removing paper, spread each of 3 layers with 1 tbsp (15 mL) marmalade each; stack layers. Top with 1 layer. Repeat with remaining layers to form 2 stacks.

● Cut stacks lengthwise into 1/2-inch (1 cm) wide slices. Cut each slice crosswise into 3 pieces. Stand pieces against side of 12-cup (3 L) glass bowl, alternating pieces so lines are at right angles to create checkerboard. Cover bottom with pieces; brush with half of the liqueur. Cover with half of the oranges.

● Whip 1/2 cup (125 mL) of the cream; fold into custard. Fold in chopped praline. Spread half over oranges. Leaving border, top with remaining cake, then liqueur. Cover with remaining oranges, then custard. Cover and refrigerate for 4 hours or for up to 1 day.

● Whip remaining cream; spread over top. Garnish with reserved praline and oranges. Makes 12 servings.

Praline, a golden nut brittle, adds a glamorous look to the top of this trifle and a bewitching taste to the custard filling. If you prefer, use 2-1/2 cups (625 mL) membrane-free orange or blood orange segments, patted dry, in place of the canned mandarins.

Per serving: about
- 535 calories
- 9 g protein
- 20 g fat
- 81 g carbohydrate

Three-Berry Fool

Don't let the name fool you — this make-ahead confection of layered cream and summer berries is dessert perfection.

Per serving: about
- 375 calories
- 3 g protein
- 32 g fat
- 21 g carbohydrate
- high source of fiber

3 cups	raspberries	750 mL
3 tbsp	icing sugar	50 mL
1-1/2 cups	whipping cream	375 mL
1 cup	sliced strawberries	250 mL
1 cup	blackberries	250 mL
	Fresh mint sprigs	

● In food processor or blender, purée 2 cups (500 mL) of the raspberries. With wooden spoon, press through fine sieve into bowl to make about 2/3 cup (150 mL) purée. Whisk in 2 tbsp (25 mL) of the sugar. Remove 1/3 cup (75 mL) and set aside.

● In bowl, whip cream with remaining sugar; fold in remaining purée.

● Spoon about 1/3 cup (75 mL) of the raspberry cream into each of four long-stemmed glasses. Top with heaping 1 tsp (5 mL) reserved purée. Scatter some of the remaining raspberries and strawberries over top. Repeat layering two more times.

● Garnish with blackberries, any remaining raspberries and strawberries and mint sprigs. *(Desserts can be covered and refrigerated for up to 3 hours.)* Makes 4 servings.

Key Lime Mousse ▶

Any time is right for a Florida fantasy, especially a lightened-up, key-lime kind.

Per serving: about
- 330 calories
- 8 g protein
- 14 g fat
- 44 g carbohydrate

2/3 cup	lime juice	150 mL
2 tbsp	granulated sugar	25 mL
2 tsp	unflavored gelatin	10 mL
1 tbsp	grated lime rind	15 mL
	Green food coloring	
1	can (10 oz/300 mL) low-fat sweetened condensed milk	1
1 cup	whipping cream	250 mL
1	lime, thinly sliced	1

● In saucepan, combine lime juice with sugar. Sprinkle with gelatin; let soften for 1 minute. Heat over medium heat, stirring, for 3 minutes or until dissolved.

● Stir in lime rind and enough drops of food coloring to tint bright green (color will soften when cream is added). Let cool to room temperature. Whisk in milk; cover and refrigerate for 15 minutes or until slightly thickened.

● In bowl, whip cream; fold into lime mixture. Spoon into parfait glasses; cover and refrigerate for at least 1 hour or until set. *(Mousse can be refrigerated for up to 24 hours.)* To serve, garnish with lime slices. Makes 6 servings.

Swirled Apricot Fool

3 cups	dried apricots (1 lb/500 g)	750 mL
1/2 cup	granulated sugar	125 mL
	Lightened Whipped Cream (recipe follows)	
1/2 cup	chopped pistachios	125 mL

● In saucepan, bring apricots and 4 cups (1 L) water to boil; cover, reduce heat and simmer for about 40 minutes or until apricots are very tender.

● In food processor, purée apricot mixture until smooth; return to saucepan. Add sugar; bring to bubbling simmer over low heat, stirring. Cook, stirring, for about 3 minutes or until sugar is dissolved; let cool. *(Dessert can be prepared to this point and refrigerated in airtight container for up to 3 days.)*

● Spoon Lightened Whipped Cream into eight chilled dessert goblets; top with apricot mixture. Swirl with handle of spoon; sprinkle with pistachios. Makes 10 servings.

LIGHTENED WHIPPED CREAM		
1-1/2 cups	low-fat plain yogurt	375 mL
1/2 cup	whipping cream	125 mL
1 tbsp	granulated sugar	15 mL
1 tbsp	orange liqueur (optional)	15 mL
1 tsp	grated orange rind	5 mL

● Spoon yogurt into cheesecloth-lined sieve set over bowl. Drain in refrigerator for about 3 hours or until reduced to about 3/4 cup (175 mL). Transfer to bowl; discard liquid. *(Drained yogurt can be refrigerated in airtight container for up to 2 days.)*

● In separate bowl, whip cream; stir about one-quarter into drained yogurt. Stir in sugar, liqueur (if using) and orange rind. Fold in remaining whipped cream. Makes 1-1/2 cups (375 mL).

Per 2 tbsp (25 mL): about
• 85 calories • 3 g protein • 7 g fat • 4 g carbohydrate

T*hick, low-fat yogurt combined with the whipped cream gives this golden fool its luscious taste — without the usual calories or grams of fat. You can also make the Lightened Whipped Cream on its own, for spooning on dishes of fresh or cooked fruit.*

Per serving: about
• 245 calories • 5 g protein
• 8 g fat • 43 g carbohydrate
• high source of fiber • good source of iron

Strawberry Pavlova

4	egg whites	4
Pinch	salt	Pinch
1 cup	granulated sugar	250 mL
1 tbsp	cornstarch	15 mL
2 tsp	vinegar	10 mL
1 tsp	finely grated orange rind	5 mL
1 tsp	vanilla	5 mL
1 cup	whipping cream	250 mL
2 tbsp	orange liqueur (optional)	25 mL
4 cups	halved strawberries	1 L

● Line baking sheet with parchment paper; draw 9-inch (23 cm) circle on paper and turn paper over. (Or line sheet with greased foil, marking circle.)

● In bowl, beat egg whites with salt until soft peaks form; gradually beat in sugar, 2 tbsp (25 mL) at a time, until stiff peaks form. Beat in cornstarch, vinegar, orange rind and vanilla. Spoon onto circle on baking sheet, building up side to form nest.

● Bake in 250°F (120°C) oven for about 1-1/2 hours or until outside is crisp and lightly golden and center is soft. Let cool on pan on rack; peel off paper. *(Meringue can be covered loosely and stored for up to 3 days.)*

● Just before serving, whip cream; beat in liqueur (if using). Spoon half of the strawberries into meringue nest; cover with whipped cream. Garnish with remaining strawberries. Makes 8 servings.

J*uicy fresh berries and softly whipped cream in a light, melt-in-your-mouth meringue — one taste, and you'll understand why this remains a summer classic.*

Per serving: about
• 230 calories • 3 g protein
• 11 g fat • 32 g carbohydrate

Show-Off Raspberry Charlotte ◀

3	eggs, separated	3
1/2 cup	granulated sugar	125 mL
1 tsp	vanilla	5 mL
1/4 tsp	cream of tartar	1 mL
3/4 cup	sifted cake-and-pastry flour	175 mL
2 tbsp	icing sugar	25 mL
	FILLING	
2	pkg (10 oz/300 g each) frozen unsweetened raspberries, thawed	2
3/4 cup	granulated sugar	175 mL
4 tsp	unflavored gelatin	20 mL
2-1/2 cups	whipping cream	625 mL
2 cups	fresh raspberries	500 mL

● Line two 17- x 11-inch (45 x 29 cm) baking sheets with parchment paper. Draw 12- x 6-inch (30 x 15 cm) rectangle and 7-inch (18 cm) disc on paper; turn paper over.

● In bowl, beat egg yolks with 1/4 cup (50 mL) of the granulated sugar for 2 minutes or until pale and thickened. Stir in vanilla.

● In separate bowl, beat egg whites with cream of tartar until soft peaks form. Gradually beat in remaining granulated sugar until stiff peaks form; fold one-third into egg yolks. Spoon another third over yolks; sift half of flour over top and fold in gently. Repeat with remaining egg whites and flour.

● Spoon batter into large piping bag. Starting at one corner of traced rectangle, pipe batter diagonally into strips, each about 6 inches (15 cm) long and just barely touching. Fill in rectangle with shorter strips to fit. Pipe batter in concentric circles, starting at center, to fill traced circles. Sprinkle icing sugar over tops.

● Bake in 325°F (160°C) oven, rotating pans halfway through baking, for 20 to 25 minutes or until puffed and golden. Let cool in pans on rack. Gently remove paper. Place circle in 8-inch (2 L) springform pan. Cut rectangle in half lengthwise; stand, puffed side out, around edge of pan, trimming if necessary.

● FILLING: In food processor, purée thawed raspberries and all but 4 tsp (20 mL) of the sugar. Press through fine sieve into bowl, extracting as much juice as possible.

● In saucepan, sprinkle gelatin over 1/3 cup (75 mL) cold water; let soften for 1 minute. Heat over low heat until gelatin dissolves; stir into purée. Refrigerate, stirring occasionally, for 1 hour or until almost set.

● In separate bowl, whip 1-1/2 cups (375 mL) of the cream; fold in one-third of the raspberry mixture. Fold in remaining raspberry mixture.

● Scatter half of the fresh raspberries over cake base. Spoon raspberry mixture over top. Cover and refrigerate for 4 hours or until set. Whip remaining cream with remaining sugar; spread on top. Top with remaining raspberries. Makes 12 servings.

A *word of warning — with frozen raspberries now widely available, this make-ahead ladyfinger-and-fruit-mousse dessert is bound to become a year-round indulgence!*

Per serving: about
- 320 calories
- 5 g protein
- 19 g fat
- 34 g carbohydrate

PITCHER-POURING CUSTARD

This is crème anglaise, the glamorous custard that pools deliciously under tarts or drizzles over fruit.

● In heavy saucepan, heat 2 cups (500 mL) milk over low heat until bubbles form around edge of pan.
● In bowl, whisk 6 egg yolks with 1/3 cup (75 mL) granulated sugar and pinch of salt; whisk in 1/2 cup (125 mL) of the milk. Stir back into pan and cook, stirring constantly with wooden spoon, until thick enough to coat spoon.
● Remove from heat; stir in dash of vanilla. Strain through fine sieve into pitcher. Let cool, stirring often to prevent skin forming on surface. Cover surface with plastic wrap; refrigerate for up to 2 days. Makes 2-1/2 cups (625 mL).

Per 1/4 cup (50 mL): about
- 90 calories • 3 g protein • 4 g fat
- 9 g carbohydrate

Orange Crème Caramel with Fruit ▼

There are two secrets to a great crème caramel — dare to cook the caramel until it's quite dark, with just the slightest hint of bitterness, and bake the custard only until the center is wobbly (otherwise, the texture will be rubbery).

Per serving: about
- 430 calories
- 6 g fat
- good source of calcium
- 10 g protein
- 87 g carbohydrate
- very high source of fiber

4	seedless oranges	4
2	pink grapefruit	2
1/2 cup	granulated sugar	125 mL
1/4 cup	water	50 mL
	Mint leaves	
	CARAMEL	
3/4 cup	granulated sugar	175 mL
1/2 cup	water	125 mL
	CUSTARD	
2 cups	milk	500 mL
1/2 cup	granulated sugar	125 mL
	Grated rind of 1 orange	
5	eggs	5
2 tsp	orange liqueur	10 mL

● CARAMEL: In heavy saucepan, dissolve sugar in 1/3 cup (75 mL) of the water over low heat. Increase heat to high; cook, without stirring, just until deep caramel color and beginning to smoke. Remove from heat. Carefully and slowly add remaining water, swirling pan. Pour into six 6-oz (175 mL) ovenproof ramekins. Refrigerate until cooled and almost set, about 30 minutes.

● CUSTARD: In heavy saucepan, combine milk, sugar and orange rind; heat over high heat just until bubbles form around edge of saucepan. In large bowl, whisk eggs; whisk in hot milk in thin steady stream. Strain into clean bowl; stir in orange liqueur. Pour over cooled caramel in ramekins.

● Set ramekins in ovenproof pan; pour in enough boiling water to come three-quarters up sides of ramekins. Cover with foil; bake in 325°F (160°C) oven for 25 to 30 minutes or until set around outside but still slightly jiggly in center. (Custard will set completely upon cooling.) Remove from water; let cool for 30 minutes. Refrigerate for 4 hours or until set enough to unmold. *(Custard can be refrigerated for up to 1 day.)*

● Being careful not to include any white pith, cut off orange and grapefruit rinds in thin strips. Drop rind into boiling water for 30 seconds; drain well. In small saucepan, bring sugar, water and orange and grapefruit rinds to simmer over medium heat; cook for 2 to 3 minutes or until sugar is dissolved and rind is translucent. *(Rind can be set aside in liquid for up to 4 hours; if liquid hardens, melt over low heat.)* Drain.

● With paring knife, cut off white pith and membrane from grapefruit and oranges. Cut sections away from inner membranes and place in bowl; toss to combine. Refrigerate until chilled. *(Fruit can be refrigerated for up to 4 hours.)*

● To serve, let custard stand at room temperature for 30 minutes. Run knife around edge of each and unmold onto plates. Surround with grapefruit, oranges and candied rind. Garnish with mint. Makes 6 servings.

Orange Mousse Angel Meringue ▲

3	egg whites	3
1/4 tsp	cream of tartar	1 mL
2/3 cup	granulated sugar	150 mL
1 tbsp	cornstarch	15 mL
	ORANGE MOUSSE FILLING	
1	pkg (0.3 oz/7 g) unflavored gelatin	1
1-1/2 cups	orange juice	75 mL
3	egg yolks	3
2 tbsp	grated orange rind	25 mL
1/2 cup	granulated sugar	125 mL
3/4 cup	chilled 2% evaporated milk	175 mL

● In bowl, beat egg whites with cream of tartar until soft peaks form. Gradually beat in sugar, 1 tbsp (15 mL) at a time, until stiff glossy peaks form. Blend in cornstarch.

● Line baking sheet with parchment paper or greased foil; spread meringue into 9-inch (23 cm) circle, forming 1-inch (2.5 cm) high rounded rim. Bake in 300°F (150°C) oven for about 1 hour or until crisp. Turn oven off; let meringue stand in oven for 12 hours. Gently peel off paper; place on serving plate.

● ORANGE MOUSSE FILLING: In bowl, sprinkle gelatin over 1/2 cup (125 mL) of the orange juice; set aside. In nonaluminum saucepan, whisk egg yolks lightly. Add orange rind, remaining orange juice and sugar; cook over medium heat, stirring constantly, for 5 to 10 minutes or until thick enough to coat back of spoon. Stir into gelatin mixture until gelatin is dissolved. Cover and refrigerate for about 15 minutes or until slightly thickened.

● In separate bowl, beat evaporated milk for 1 minute or until thick and foamy; fold into gelatin mixture until combined. Spoon into meringue shell; cover and refrigerate for about 30 minutes or until set. *(Pie can be refrigerated for up to 8 hours.)* Makes 8 servings.

A *whipped evaporated-milk filling delivers all the creaminess — and a lot less fat — in this heavenly dessert. Garnish with twists of orange, mint sprigs and a dusting of cocoa powder.*

Per serving: about
- 190 calories
- 5 g protein
- 3 g fat
- 38 g carbohydrate

TIP: The evaporated millk must be well chilled for it to whip.

Lemon Semifreddo with Raspberry Coulis ▲

Pastry chef Joanne Yolles created this refreshing lemony dessert. It's an excellent choice for entertaining since it can be made up to two weeks ahead.

Per serving: about
- 250 calories
- 15 g fat
- 4 g protein
- 28 g carbohydrate

TIP: Cut the semifreddo right after it comes out of the freezer and chill plates before serving.

4	eggs, separated	4
1 cup	granulated sugar	250 mL
3 tbsp	finely grated lemon rind	50 mL
1/2 cup	lemon juice	125 mL
1-1/2 cups	whipping cream	375 mL
	Raspberry Coulis (recipe follows)	

● Line 9- x 5-inch (2 L) loaf pan with waxed or parchment paper to extend 1 inch (2.5 cm) above edge. Set aside.

● In large bowl, combine egg yolks, 1/4 cup (50 mL) of the sugar, and lemon rind and juice; place over saucepan of simmering water and cook, whisking constantly, for about 8 minutes or until thickened. Place plastic wrap directly on surface; refrigerate for about 30 minutes or until cold. In bowl, whip cream; fold into cold lemon mixture.

● In separate bowl, beat egg whites until soft peaks form; gradually beat in remaining sugar, 2 tbsp (25 mL) at a time, until stiff glossy peaks form. Fold one-quarter into lemon mixture; fold in remaining egg whites.

Turn into prepared pan, smoothing top. Freeze for about 6 hours or until firm. Wrap in plastic wrap or foil and freeze overnight.

● To serve, run knife between paper and pan of semifreddo; turn out onto cutting board and remove paper. Slice and arrange on plates; let stand for 5 to 10 minutes or until softened slightly. Serve with Raspberry Coulis. Makes 10 servings.

RASPBERRY COULIS		
2 cups	unsweetened raspberries (fresh or thawed)	500 mL
1 tbsp	lemon juice	15 mL
3 tbsp	granulated sugar	50 mL

● In blender or food processor, purée raspberries and lemon juice until smooth; strain through fine sieve into airtight container. Stir in sugar. (*Coulis can be refrigerated for up to 3 days.*) Makes 1 cup (250 mL).

Per tbsp (15 mL): about
- 15 calories • trace protein • trace fat • 3 g carbohydrate

Citrus Semifreddo with Orange Sauce

1 cup	granulated sugar	250 mL
1/4 cup	butter	50 mL
1 tbsp	grated orange rind	15 mL
3/4 cup	orange juice	175 mL
1 tsp	grated lemon rind	5 mL
1/4 cup	lemon juice	50 mL
3	eggs, beaten	3
1-1/2 cups	whipping cream	375 mL
	ORANGE SAUCE	
2 cups	orange juice	500 mL
1/2 cup	granulated sugar	125 mL
1 tbsp	cornstarch	15 mL
1 tbsp	lemon juice	15 mL

● In heavy saucepan, whisk together sugar, butter, orange rind and juice, lemon rind and juice and eggs; cook over medium heat, whisking constantly, for about 10 minutes or just until boiling. Transfer to bowl; let cool to room temperature.

● In separate bowl, whip cream; fold into orange mixture. Spoon into bowl lined with plastic wrap. Freeze for at least 4 hours or until firm, or for up to 12 hours.

● ORANGE SAUCE: Meanwhile, in saucepan, whisk together orange juice, sugar, cornstarch and lemon juice; cook over medium heat, stirring often, for about 10 minutes or until thickened. Refrigerate for at least 2 hours or until chilled. (*Sauce can be refrigerated in airtight container for up to 2 days.*)

● To serve, invert bowl onto platter; remove bowl and plastic wrap. Slice into wedges. Serve with Orange Sauce. Makes 8 servings.

A *tangy orange-and-lemon curd blends with cream for a spectacular frozen dessert that looks and tastes like a lot of work — but isn't. Place wedges on chilled plates and let soften for a few minutes before serving with the sauce and/or orange segments.*

Per serving: about
- 415 calories
- 4 g protein
- 23 g fat
- 50 g carbohydrate

Frozen Apricot Soufflés

1-1/2 cups	dried apricots (8 oz/250 g)	375 mL
1/2 cup	granulated sugar	125 mL
1/4 cup	orange juice	50 mL
1-1/2 cups	whipping cream	375 mL

● In saucepan, stir together apricots, 1-1/2 cups (375 mL) water, sugar and orange juice; bring to boil. Reduce heat, cover and simmer until very soft, about 25 minutes.

● In food processor, purée apricot mixture until smooth. Transfer to bowl; refrigerate until cool.

● In separate bowl, whip cream. Stir one-quarter into apricot mixture; fold in remaining whipped cream. Spoon enough of the mixture into each of eight 4-oz (125 mL) soufflé dishes to fill almost to top.

● Cut eight 10- x 1-inch (25 x 2.5 cm) strips of parchment or waxed paper; place around inside of each dish to form collar, inserting into mixture slightly. Spoon in remaining apricot mixture; make decorative swirls on top. Freeze until solid, about 4 hours. (*Soufflés can be wrapped well and stored in freezer for up to 1 week.*) Discard collars to serve. Makes 8 servings.

S *pecial-occasion desserts are much less fuss when you make them ahead in individual servings.*

Per serving: about
- 290 calories
- 2 g protein
- 16 g fat
- 38 g carbohydrate

Peach Ice Cream ▼

Fruit ice creams can be made simply with ripe, juicy fruit, cream and sugar — or, in the French tradition, with a custard base, as here.

Per 1/2 cup (125 mL): about
- 285 calories
- 4 g protein
- 17 g fat
- 32 g carbohydrate

6	large peaches (1-1/2 lb/750 g)	6
1/4 cup	granulated sugar	50 mL
	CUSTARD	
3	egg yolks	3
1/3 cup	granulated sugar	75 mL
1 cup	light cream	250 mL
1/2 cup	whipping cream	125 mL
1-1/2 tsp	vanilla	7 mL

● CUSTARD: In bowl, whisk egg yolks with sugar for 2 minutes or until pale and thickened; set aside. In saucepan, heat light cream over medium-high heat just until bubbles form around edge; gradually whisk into yolk mixture.

● Return egg mixture to pan; cook over low heat, stirring constantly, for about 12 minutes or until thick enough to coat back of wooden spoon. Immediately strain through sieve into large bowl. Stir in whipping cream and vanilla. Let cool to room temperature. Place waxed paper directly on surface; refrigerate for at least 2 hours or until chilled or for up to 24 hours.

● Peel and slice peaches. In bowl, combine peaches with sugar; let stand for about 20 minutes or until juicy. In food processor or blender, purée peaches to make about 2 cups (500 mL). Fold into chilled custard.

● Pour into shallow metal pan; cover and freeze for 3 to 4 hours or until almost firm. Break up into chunks; transfer to food processor and purée until smooth.

● Transfer to chilled airtight container; freeze for 1 hour or until firm. (Alternatively, freeze in ice-cream machine according to manufacturer's instructions.) *(Ice cream can be stored in freezer for up to 3 days.)* Transfer to refrigerator 30 minutes before serving. Makes about 3 cups (750 mL).

VARIATION
● RED PLUM ICE CREAM: Omit peach mixture. In saucepan, combine 3 cups (750 mL) sliced (unpeeled) red plums (about 5), 1/4 cup (50 mL) water and 2 tbsp (25 mL) granulated sugar; simmer over low heat for 20 minutes or until tender. Purée, then chill; fold into custard.

TIPS
● Homemade ice cream is best made in a small batch and eaten within 3 days.
● You can add a tablespoon (15 mL) liqueur to purée: orange liqueur to peaches; cassis to plums.

Strawberry Ice Cream

3	egg yolks	3
1/2 cup	granulated sugar	125 mL
1-1/2 cups	light cream	375 mL
1 tsp	vanilla	5 mL
2 cups	strawberries	500 mL

● In bowl, whisk egg yolks with sugar until pale and thickened; set aside. In saucepan, heat cream over medium heat just until bubbles form around edge; gradually whisk into yolk mixture.

● Return egg mixture to pan; cook, whisking constantly, for 3 to 5 minutes or until thick enough to coat back of wooden spoon. Stir in vanilla. Immediately strain through sieve into large bowl; let cool to room temperature.

Place waxed paper directly on surface; refrigerate for at least 2 hours or until chilled.

● In food processor, purée strawberries; stir into chilled cream mixture. Pour into shallow metal pan; cover and freeze for 3 to 4 hours or until almost firm. Break up into chunks; transfer to food processor and purée until smooth.

● Transfer to chilled airtight container; freeze for 1 hour or until firm. (Alternatively, freeze in ice-cream machine according to manufacturer's instructions.) *(Ice cream can be stored in freezer for up to 3 days.)* Transfer to refrigerator 30 minutes before serving. Makes about 4 cups (1 L).

S*tore-bought strawberry ice cream can't match the flavor of freshly picked strawberries in this easy homemade version.*

Per 1/2 cup (125 mL): about
- 170 calories
- 10 g fat
- 3 g protein
- 17 g carbohydrate

White Chocolate Cranberry Swirl Ice Cream

1 cup	cranberries (fresh or frozen)	250 mL
1/2 cup	granulated sugar	125 mL
6	egg yolks	6
2 cups	light cream	500 mL
6 oz	white chocolate, chopped	175 g
1 cup	whipping cream	250 mL
1 tsp	vanilla	5 mL

● In saucepan, bring cranberries, 2 tbsp (25 mL) of the sugar and 1/4 cup (50 mL) water to boil; reduce heat and simmer, stirring occasionally, for 5 minutes or until thickened. Using rubber spatula, press through sieve set over small bowl; cover and refrigerate purée for 1 hour or until chilled. *(Purée can be refrigerated for up to 1 day.)*

● In large bowl, whisk egg yolks with remaining sugar; set aside. In saucepan, heat light cream over medium-high heat just until bubbles form around edge; gradually whisk into yolk mixture. Return egg mixture to pan; cook over medium-low heat, stirring constantly, for about 10 minutes until thick enough to coat back of wooden spoon.

● Immediately strain through sieve into large bowl. Add white chocolate; stir until melted. Stir in whipping cream and vanilla. Let cool to room temperature. Place waxed paper directly on surface; refrigerate for at least 2 hours or until chilled. *(Ice cream can be prepared to this point and refrigerated for up to 24 hours.)*

● Pour into shallow metal pan; cover and freeze for 3 to 4 hours or until almost firm. Break up into chunks; transfer to food processor and purée until smooth. (Alternatively, freeze in ice-cream machine according to manufacturer's instructions until frozen yet still soft enough to swirl.)

● Transfer one-quarter of the ice-cream mixture into chilled 6-cup (1.5 L) plastic freezer container. Using rubber spatula, swirl in one-quarter of the cranberry purée. Repeat 3 times. Cover and freeze for 1 hour or until firm. *(Ice cream can be stored in freezer for up to 5 days.)* Transfer to refrigerator 30 minutes before serving. Makes about 5 cups (1.25 L).

W*hite chocolate is so sweet and creamy that it needs to be cut with a tart fruit such as cranberries.*

Per 1/2 cup (125 mL): about
- 340 calories
- 26 g fat
- 5 g protein
- 23 carbohydrate

Fresh Pear Ice Cream

When Julia Child came for lunch in the Test Kitchen, this is the fresh pear ice cream associate food director Daphna Rabinovitch made in her honor.

Per 1/2 cup (125 mL): about
• 290 calories   • 3 g protein
• 19 g fat   • 30 g carbohydrate

4	egg yolks	4
1-1/2 cups	whipping cream	375 mL
3/4 cup	granulated sugar	175 mL
1 tbsp	pear liqueur (optional)	15 mL
1/2 tsp	vanilla	2 mL
3	ripe pears (about 1-1/2 lb/750 g)	3

● In bowl, whisk egg yolks until pale and thickened; set aside. In saucepan, combine 1 cup (250 mL) of the cream with sugar; cook over medium heat, stirring, for about 5 minutes or until sugar is dissolved. Gradually whisk into egg yolks, whisking constantly.

● Return egg mixture to pan; cook over medium-low heat, stirring constantly, for about 12 minutes or until thick enough to coat back of wooden spoon. Immediately strain through fine sieve into large bowl. Stir in remaining cream, pear liqueur (if using) and vanilla.

● Meanwhile, peel, core and coarsely chop pears. In saucepan, combine pears with 1/4 cup (50 mL) water; cook over medium heat for 5 minutes or until heated through. In blender or food processor, purée pear mixture to make about 1-1/2 cups (375 mL). Stir into custard. Let cool to room temperature. Place waxed paper directly on surface; refrigerate for at least 2 hours or until chilled.

● Pour into shallow metal pan; cover and freeze for 3 to 4 hours or until almost firm. Break up into chunks; transfer to food processor and purée until smooth.

● Transfer to chilled airtight container; freeze for 1 hour or until firm. (Alternatively, freeze in ice-cream machine according to manufacturer's instructions.) *(Ice cream can be stored in freezer for up to 3 days.)* Transfer to refrigerator 30 minutes before serving. Makes about 4 cups (1 L).

TIP: You must have perfectly ripe, fragrant pears for any cold dessert, since lower temperatures diminish flavors. Bartletts are the flavor champions, but you have to buy them ahead of time and let ripen at room temperature.

THE SCOOP ON SERVING SORBETS

● When serving sorbet or any other frozen dessert, chill the bowls, cups, stemmed glasses or plates that will hold the offering.
● Instead of serving one large scoop of sorbet, scoop out a variety and arrange sorbets by color and taste — for example, strawberry rhubarb, mango and kiwi or, for a variety of pinks, pink grapefruit, plum and raspberry. Incorporate ice creams that mix and match with the sorbets — strawberry ice cream with sorbet of the same flavor, bought vanilla or dark chocolate with berry sorbets.
● Pluck mint, lemon verbena or scented geranium leaves for garnish. Edible flowers or flower petals — especially violets, violas, geraniums and nasturtiums — add a touch of beauty to a dessert.
● Serve sorbets and ice creams with complementary fruits — a scatter of sliced strawberries over Strawberry Rhubarb Sorbet, peaches over Peach Ice Cream (p. 48).
● Homemade frozen confections should be made and enjoyed as soon as possible.

Pink Grapefruit Sorbet ▼

4	large red grapefruit	4
3/4 cup	granulated sugar	175 mL

● Grate enough rind from grapefruit to make 1 tbsp (15 mL). Squeeze out juice and strain through fine sieve to make 3-1/2 cups (875 mL). Set aside.

● In saucepan, stir together sugar, grapefruit rind and 3/4 cup (175 mL) water until sugar is dissolved. Bring to boil; cook for 5 minutes. Strain through sieve into bowl; let cool. Stir in grapefruit juice.

● Transfer to shallow metal pan; cover and freeze for 3 to 4 hours or until almost firm. Break up into chunks; transfer to food processor and purée until smooth.

● Pour into chilled airtight container; freeze for 1 hour or until firm. (Alternatively, freeze in ice-cream machine according to manufacturer's instructions.) *(Sorbet can be stored in freezer for up to 1 day.)* Makes about 4 cups (1 L).

If you're serving a multi-course dinner and a sorbet is called for to refresh the palate, a small scoop of this tangy flavor is just right.

Per 1/2 cup (125 mL): about
- 115 calories
- trace fat
- 1 g protein
- 29 g carbohydrate

Strawberry Rhubarb Sorbet ▼

3 cups	chopped rhubarb (fresh or thawed)	750 mL
1 cup	granulated sugar	250 mL
2 cups	strawberries (fresh or thawed)	500 mL

● In saucepan, cook rhubarb with 1/4 cup (50 mL) water over low heat for about 10 minutes or until juices are released. Stir in sugar. Increase heat to medium; cover and cook for about 5 minutes or until tender. Let cool.

● In food processor, purée rhubarb with strawberries until smooth. Pour into shallow metal pan; cover and freeze for 3 to 4 hours or until almost firm. Break up into chunks; transfer to food processor and purée until smooth.

● Transfer to chilled airtight container; freeze for 1 hour or until firm.

(Alternatively, freeze in ice-cream machine according to manufacturer's instructions.) *(Sorbet can be stored in freezer for up to 1 day.)* Makes about 4 cups (1 L).

Vibrant with summer-fresh flavors and colors, this sorbet is so rich and smooth you'll think you're eating ice cream!

Per 1/2 cup (125 mL): about
- 120 calories
- trace fat
- 1 g protein
- 29 g carbohydrate

Pink Grapefruit and Strawberry Rhubarb Sorbets

Pies and Pastries

When it comes to celebrating the pleasures of fruit, nothing beats a hot-from-the-oven pie — tender, flaky pastry bursting with the season's best apples, peaches, pears, rhubarb or berries. From classic Canadian to trendy and new, here's our pick of pies and tarts at their most pleasing.

Best-Ever Apple Pie ▶

We call this our best because the apple filling is neither too tart nor too sweet, and the pastry is so easy to make. It's adapted from Bride's Pastry, *a recipe that food writer Helen Gougeon included in* Good Food, *published almost forty years ago.*

Per serving: about
- 470 calories
- 24 g fat
- 5 g protein
- 59 g carbohydrate

	Pastry for 9-inch (23 cm) double-crust pie (recipe follows)	
	FILLING	
8 cups	thinly sliced peeled tart apples (2-2/3 lb/1.35 kg)	2 L
2 tbsp	lemon juice	25 mL
1/2 cup	granulated sugar	125 mL
3 tbsp	all-purpose flour	50 mL
1/2 tsp	cinnamon	2 mL
	GLAZE	
1	egg yolk	1
2 tsp	granulated sugar	10 mL

● On well-floured surface, roll out 1 of the pastry discs into 13-inch (33 cm) circle. Fit into 9-inch (23 cm) pie plate; trim edge even with plate.

● FILLING: In large bowl, toss apples with lemon juice. Stir together sugar, flour and cinnamon; sprinkle over apples and toss until coated. Scrape into pie shell. Brush pastry rim with water.

● Roll out remaining pastry to same size circle. Drape over apples; trim, leaving 3/4-inch (2 cm) overhang. Fold overhang under bottom pastry rim; seal and flute edge. Cut steam vents in center.

● GLAZE: Whisk yolk with 1 tbsp (15 mL) water; brush over top. Sprinkle with sugar. Bake in bottom third of 425°F (220°C) oven for 15 minutes. Reduce heat to 350°F (180°C); bake for 40 minutes or until golden, filling is bubbly and apples are soft when pierced with knife through vent. Let cool on rack. Makes 8 servings.

	PASTRY	
3/4 cup	shortening	175 mL
3 tbsp	butter, softened	50 mL
2-1/4 cups	all-purpose flour	550 mL
3/4 tsp	salt	4 mL
1/2 cup	ice water	125 mL

● In bowl, beat shortening with butter until smooth; stir in flour and salt until coarse and ragged looking. Pour in water all at once; stir until loose dough forms.

● With floured hands, press into 2 balls. On well-floured surface, gently press each into 3/4-inch (2 cm) thick disc. Wrap and refrigerate for at least 1 hour or until chilled. *(Discs can be refrigerated for up to 5 days or frozen for up to 2 weeks.)* Makes pastry for 1 double-crust or 2 single-crust pies.

PERFECT DOUBLE-CRUST FRUIT PIES

Type of Pie	Prepared Fruit	Granulated Sugar	All-purpose Flour	Flavorings
Blueberry	5 cups (1.25 L)	3/4 cup (175 mL)	1/4 cup (50 mL)	1/2 tsp (2 mL) each grated lemon rind and cinnamon
Peach	5 cups (1.25 L), peeled and sliced	3/4 cup (175 mL)	1/4 cup (50 mL)	2 tbsp (25 mL) chopped candied ginger
Plum	5 cups (1.25 L), quartered if large, halved if small	1 cup (250 mL)	1/4 cup (50 mL)	1/2 tsp (2 mL) cinnamon
Raspberry	4 cups (1 L)	1 cup (250 mL)	3 tbsp (50 mL)	none needed
Apple	6 cups (1.5 L), peeled and sliced	3/4 cup (175 mL)	1 tbsp (15 mL)	1/4 tsp (1 mL) nutmeg and 1/2 tsp (2 mL) cinnamon
Sour Cherry	4 cups (1 L) pitted	1 cup (250 mL)	1/4 cup (50 mL)	1/2 tsp (2 mL) almond extract

● Line 9-inch (23 cm) pie plate with pastry.

● In large bowl, combine prepared fruit, sugar, flour, 1 tbsp (15 mL) lemon juice and flavoring (see chart for amounts).

● Fill pastry shell with fruit mixture; dot filling with 1 tbsp (15 mL) butter.

● Moisten edge of bottom crust. Cover with top crust. Trim and flute edge. Cut steam vents. Brush top with milk or cream; sprinkle lightly with granulated sugar.

● Bake in bottom third of 425°F (220°C) oven for 15 minutes; reduce heat to 350°F (180°C) and bake for 35 to 45 minutes longer or until fruit is tender, filling is thickened and crust golden.

FREEZING PIES

● You can freeze well-wrapped unbaked fruit pies for up to 4 months, with the following changes: increase the amount of flour in each pie by 1 tbsp (15 mL) and don't cut steam vents until just before baking.

● Bake still-frozen pies in 450°F (230°C) oven for 15 minutes; reduce heat to 375°F (190°C) and bake for up to 60 minutes longer or until filling is thickened and crust golden brown.

EASY GLAZING

A pie with a beautiful gloss and golden color is especially appealing. There are several ways to get a professional-looking glaze.

● Whisk together an egg yolk with 1-1/2 tsp (7 mL) cream for a deep-gold color. Milk or water can replace the cream, but the glaze will be less golden. Or, use a whole beaten egg (the white adds particular gloss), cream or milk. Just before baking, brush the top pastry with choice of glaze.

● For fruit pies, especially cherry and apple, and wintertime pies such as raisin, sprinkle granulated sugar over the glaze to make the pie glitter.

A la Mode Bumbleberry Pie

	Pastry for 9-inch (23 cm) double-crust pie (see Pastry, p. 52)	
1 cup	chopped rhubarb	250 mL
2 cups	chopped peeled apples	500 mL
1 cup	blackberries	250 mL
1 cup	raspberries	250 mL
3/4 cup	granulated sugar	175 mL
4 tsp	all-purpose flour	20 mL
4 tsp	cornstarch	20 mL
4 tsp	butter	20 mL
1 tbsp	lemon juice	15 mL

● On lightly floured surface, roll out half of the pastry and fit into 9-inch (23 cm) pie plate; set aside.

● In microwaveable measure, microwave rhubarb at High for 50 seconds or until slightly softened. (Or steam in steamer for 3 minutes.)

● In large bowl, combine rhubarb, apples, blackberries and raspberries. Combine sugar, flour and cornstarch; toss gently with fruit mixture. Spoon into pie shell; dot with butter and sprinkle with lemon juice.

● Roll out remaining pastry; moisten rim of pastry shell and fit pastry over filling, pressing gently to rim. Trim and flute edge; cut steam vents in top.

● Bake in bottom third of 425°F (220°C) oven for 15 minutes; reduce heat to 350°F (180°C) and bake for 35 minutes longer or until pastry is golden and filling is bubbly. Let cool on rack. Makes 8 servings.

A la Mode *means "with ice cream," and this pie is particularly delicious served with a scoop of your favorite ice cream.*

Per serving: about
- 340 calories
- 16 g fat
- 3 g protein
- 47 g carbohydrate

Apple Ginger Streusel Pie

	Pastry for 9-inch (23 cm) single-crust pie (see Pastry, p. 52)	
1-1/2 tsp	chopped crystallized ginger	7 mL
6	apples	6
1/3 cup	packed brown sugar	75 mL
1/4 cup	whipping cream	50 mL
	STREUSEL	
1/4 cup	all-purpose flour	50 mL
2 tbsp	packed brown sugar	25 mL
2 tbsp	butter	25 mL
1 tbsp	chopped crystallized ginger	15 mL

● STREUSEL: In bowl, stir flour with sugar; using pastry blender or two knives, cut in butter until crumbly. Stir in ginger. Set aside.

● On lightly floured surface, roll out pastry and fit into 9-inch (23 cm) pie plate; trim and flute edge. Sprinkle ginger over bottom.

● Peel, core and cut apples into eighths; toss with sugar. Arrange wedges upright on ends at 45-degree angle in concentric circles in shell. Pour cream over apples; sprinkle with streusel.

● Bake in bottom third of 425°F (220°C) oven for 15 minutes. Reduce heat to 375°F (190°C); bake for 1 hour or until apples are softened and topping is golden. Let cool on rack. Makes 8 servings.

A *crumbly golden brown topping and moist apple-rich filling make this homey pie irresistible.*

Per serving: about
- 290 calories
- 13 g fat
- 2 g protein
- 41 g carbohydrate

Peach Blueberry Crumble Pie

Peaches and blueberries make perfect partners, especially when crowned with a golden crumb topping.

Per serving: about
- 450 calories
- 21 g fat
- 5 g protein
- 63 g carbohydrate

1-1/2 cups	all-purpose flour	375 mL
1/2 tsp	salt	2 mL
1/4 cup	butter, cubed	50 mL
1/4 cup	cold shortening, cubed	50 mL
1	egg yolk	1
1 tsp	white vinegar	5 mL
	Ice water	
	FILLING	
5 cups	thickly sliced peeled peaches (about 8)	1.25 L
1 cup	blueberries	250 mL
1 tsp	grated lemon rind	5 mL
1 tbsp	lemon juice	15 mL
1/3 cup	granulated sugar	75 mL
1/4 cup	all-purpose flour	50 mL
1/2 tsp	cinnamon	2 mL
	TOPPING	
1/2 cup	packed brown sugar	125 mL
1/2 cup	all-purpose flour	125 mL
Pinch	cinnamon	Pinch
1/3 cup	butter	75 mL

● In large bowl, stir flour with salt; using pastry blender or two knives, cut in butter and shortening until in fine crumbs with a few larger pieces.

● In measuring cup, beat egg yolk with vinegar; add enough ice water to make 1/3 cup (75 mL). Stirring briskly with fork, sprinkle over flour mixture, 1 tbsp (15 mL) at a time, until dough holds together. Press into disc; wrap and refrigerate for 30 minutes.

● On lightly floured surface, roll out pastry and fit into deep 9-inch (23 cm) pie plate; trim and flute edge. Set aside.

● FILLING: In large bowl, toss together peaches, blueberries and lemon rind and juice. Stir together sugar, flour and cinnamon; sprinkle over fruit and toss to coat. Spoon into pie shell.

● TOPPING: In bowl, stir together sugar, flour and cinnamon; using pastry blender or two knives, cut in butter until crumbly. Sprinkle over filling.

● Place on rimmed baking sheet; bake in bottom third of 425°F (220°C) oven for 15 minutes. Reduce heat to 350°F (180°C); bake for about 50 minutes longer or until fruit is tender, filling is bubbly and topping is golden. Let cool on rack. Makes 8 servings.

TIP: You can refrigerate pastry for up to 3 days or freeze for up to 3 months; thaw if necessary. Let stand at room temperature for 15 minutes before rolling out.

Berry Cream Pie ▲

1-1/2 cups	whipping cream	375 mL
1-1/2 cups	2% milk	375 mL
1/2 cup	granulated sugar	125 mL
1/3 cup	cornstarch	75 mL
2 tsp	all-purpose flour	10 mL
1/2 tsp	salt	2 mL
1 tbsp	orange liqueur, rum or brandy (optional)	15 mL
3	egg yolks, lightly beaten	3
2 tbsp	butter	25 mL
1 tbsp	vanilla	15 mL
2 oz	white chocolate, coarsely chopped	60 g
1	baked 9-inch (23 cm) single-crust pie shell	1
1-1/2 cups	raspberries	375 mL
1-1/2 cups	blueberries	375 mL
	TOPPING	
1 cup	whipping cream	250 mL
1-1/2 tsp	granulated sugar	7 mL

● In saucepan, heat cream with milk over medium-high heat until bubbles form around edge of pan. In bowl, combine sugar, cornstarch, flour and salt; gradually whisk in 1 cup (250 mL) of the milk mixture, whisking constantly until smooth. Return to saucepan; stir in liqueur (if using). Cook, whisking constantly, for 3 to 5 minutes or until bubbly and thickened.

● Whisk one-quarter of the hot mixture into egg yolks; whisk back into pan. Reduce heat to low; simmer, whisking, for 1 minute. Remove from heat; whisk in butter and vanilla. Pour into bowl. Place waxed paper directly on surface; refrigerate for about 4 hours or until set.

● In bowl over hot (not boiling) water, melt white chocolate. Brush over pie shell. Scatter 3/4 cup (175 mL) each of the raspberries and blueberries over chocolate. Spoon filling over top, spreading gently.

● TOPPING: In bowl, whip cream with sugar; spread or pipe over filling. Arrange remaining berries decoratively over top. Makes 6 to 8 servings.

White chocolate seals the crust of this lusciously creamy berry pie. Garnish with white chocolate curls, if desired.

Per each of 8 servings: about
- 575 calories
- 7 g protein
- 42 g fat
- 44 g carbohydrate

TIP: To bake pie shell, chill pasrty-lined pie plate for 30 minutes. Prick base with fork. Line with foil: weigh down with pie weights. Bake in 375°F (190°C) oven for 20 minutes. Remove foil and weights. Prick again if puffed. Bake for 10 to 15 minutes or until golden.

Rhubarb Strawberry Pie with Pastry Hearts

Barbara Gordon created this masterpiece of a spring fruit pie.

Per each of 10 servings: about
- 395 calories
- 3 g protein
- 24 g fat
- 44 g carbohydrate

2 cups	all-purpose flour	500 mL
1 tsp	grated orange rind	5 mL
1/2 tsp	salt	2 mL
1-1/4 cups	unsalted butter	300 mL
1/4 cup	ice water (approx)	50 mL
	FILLING	
1 cup	granulated sugar	250 mL
2 tbsp	quick-cooking tapioca	25 mL
2 tsp	cornstarch	10 mL
1/4 tsp	each salt and grated nutmeg	1 mL
3-1/2 cups	chopped rhubarb (1-inch/ 2.5 cm chunks), about 1 lb/500 g	875 mL
1/4 cup	orange juice	50 mL
1-1/2 cups	coarsely sliced strawberries	375 mL
1 tbsp	unsalted butter	15 mL

● In large bowl, combine flour, orange rind and salt; with pastry blender or two knives, cut in butter until mixture resembles fine crumbs with a few larger pieces. Stirring briskly with fork, sprinkle with water, 1 tbsp (15 mL) at a time, and adding up to 2 tbsp (25 mL) more if necessary to make dough hold together. Press into 2 balls; flatten into discs. Wrap and refrigerate for 30 minutes. *(Pastry can be refrigerated for up to 5 days.)*

● On lightly floured surface, roll out 1 of the pastry discs and fit into 10-inch (25 cm) pie plate; trim, leaving 1/2-inch (1 cm) overhang. Fold overhang under; flute edge. Roll out remaining pastry; with 2-1/2-inch (6 cm) heart-shaped cookie cutter, cut out 24 hearts.

● FILLING: In large bowl, blend together sugar, tapioca, cornstarch, salt and nutmeg. Add rhubarb; toss to coat. Stir in orange juice. Spoon into pie shell. Scatter strawberries over top; dot with butter. Arrange heart cutouts attractively over top.

● Bake in bottom third of 425°F (220°C) oven for 15 minutes. Reduce heat to 350°F (180°C); bake for 30 to 35 minutes longer or until pastry is golden and filling is bubbly. Let cool on rack. Makes 8 to 10 servings.

HOW TO ROLL OUT PASTRY

1 Roll out pastry on a well-floured pastry cloth or surface and use a stockinette-covered or well-floured rolling pin.

2 Roll dough from center, turning pin to roll in all directions and lifting pin at edge to maintain even thickness.

3 Roll dough loosely around rolling pin; unroll loosely onto pie plate. Pat and nudge into place, but avoid stretching the dough.

4 Trim top pastry about 3/4 inch (2 cm) from edge of bottom pastry. Gently lift bottom pastry and fold overhang under. Press together to seal. Tilt sealed pastry rim up from pie plate at 15-degree angle.

5 To crimp the edge, position hand on outside of tilted pastry on rim. Using thumb and bent index finger, gently twist pastry to form scalloped edge.

6 Use a sharp knife to trim pastry and cut steam vents.

Sunburnt Lemon Pie ▲

1 cup	all-purpose flour	250 mL
1/4 cup	granulated sugar	50 mL
1/3 cup	butter	75 mL
1	egg	1
1 tsp	grated orange rind	5 mL
1 tbsp	orange juice	15 mL
	LEMON FILLING	
6	eggs	6
3/4 cup	granulated sugar	175 mL
3/4 cup	whipping cream	175 mL
1 tsp	grated lemon rind	5 mL
1/2 cup	lemon juice	125 mL
2 tsp	vanilla	10 mL

● In food processor, combine flour with sugar; using on/off motion, cut in butter until mixture resembles coarse meal.

● Combine egg, orange rind and juice; add all at once to flour mixture and mix just until ball forms. Wrap and refrigerate for 20 minutes.

● Press pastry into greased 11-inch (28 cm) flan pan; place on baking sheet. Line with foil or parchment paper; fill with pie weights or dried beans. Bake in 350°F (180°C) oven for about 20 minutes or until center is set. Remove weights and foil.

● LEMON FILLING: Meanwhile, in bowl, whisk eggs with all but 1 tbsp (15 mL) sugar; whisk in cream, lemon rind and juice and vanilla until smooth. Pour into pie shell; bake for 30 minutes. Let cool.

● Sprinkle with remaining sugar. Cover edge with foil; broil for about 3 minutes or until sugar is dark brown. Let cool on rack. Makes 8 servings.

T*his crackle-topped lemon tart is the creation of Pierre Delacôte. Serve on extra lemon curl drizzled with raspberry coulis.*

Per serving: about
- 370 calories
- 8 g protein
- 20 g fat
- 40 g carbohydrate

Chocolate Pear Tart ▶

This spectacular caramelized tart requires several steps, but most can be done ahead — and the end result is worth it!

Per each of 12 servings: about
- 430 calories
- 4 g protein
- 15 g fat
- 73 g carbohydrate

	Tart Shell (recipe follows)	
	PASTRY CREAM	
3	egg yolks	3
1/4 cup	granulated sugar	50 mL
2 tbsp	all-purpose flour	25 mL
1 cup	milk	250 mL
1/2 tsp	vanilla	2 mL
	POACHED PEARS	
7	firm ripe pears (Anjou or Bartlett)	7
1-1/2 cups	granulated sugar	375 mL
	Strip of lemon rind	
1/4 cup	lemon juice	50 mL
2 tbsp	Poire William liqueur (optional)	25 mL
	CHOCOLATE GANACHE	
1/3 cup	whipping cream	75 mL
3 oz	semisweet chocolate, finely chopped	90 g
	GLAZE AND GARNISH	
1 tbsp	granulated sugar	15 mL
1/2 cup	apricot jam	125 mL
1 tbsp	water	15 mL
	Chocolate shavings	
	Icing sugar	

● PASTRY CREAM: In bowl, whisk egg yolks with sugar until thickened and cream-colored; whisk in flour until smooth. In heavy saucepan, bring milk to boil; pour into egg mixture in thin, steady stream, stirring constantly. Strain back into saucepan; cook over medium heat, whisking constantly, until boiling. Cook, whisking, for 1 minute; remove from heat and stir in vanilla. Transfer to bowl. Place plastic wrap directly on surface; refrigerate for about 1 hour or until chilled. (*Pastry cream can be refrigerated in airtight container for up to 3 days.*)

● POACHED PEARS: Peel, halve and core pears. In shallow nonaluminum skillet, combine sugar, 4 cups (1 L) water, lemon rind and juice, and Poire William (if using); bring to boil. Add pears; cover with waxed paper. Reduce heat to medium-low; simmer for 15 to 20 minutes or just until pears are tender. Let cool in liquid. (*Pears can be refrigerated in liquid in airtight container for up to 3 days.*)

● CHOCOLATE GANACHE: In small saucepan, bring cream to boil; pour over chocolate in bowl. Let stand for 2 minutes; whisk gently until smooth. Pour into baked tart shell, spreading evenly. Refrigerate for about 30 minutes or until completely set.

● Spread pastry cream over ganache. With slotted spoon, remove pears to paper towels. Score outsides crosswise, making 1/8-inch (3 mm) deep cuts. Pat dry with paper towels. Arrange flat side down with tips toward center around outside of tart. Place 2 or 3 halves in center. Bake in 350°F (180°C) oven for 30 to 35 minutes or until pastry cream is set. Let cool on rack.

● GLAZE AND GARNISH: Remove ring from tart pan; place tart on upside-down baking sheet. Place ring upside down over tart to cover crust. Sprinkle sugar over pears. Broil about 8 inches (20 cm) from heat for about 5 minutes or until sugar caramelizes.

● Heat jam with water until melted; strain if desired. Brush over tart. Arrange chocolate shavings around rim of tart; dust with icing sugar. Serve at room temperature. Makes 10 to 12 servings.

TART SHELL		
1-1/2 cups	sifted cake-and-pastry flour	375 mL
1/4 cup	granulated sugar	50 mL
1/2 cup	unsalted butter, cut in bits	125 mL
1	egg, lightly beaten	1

● In food processor fitted with metal blade, blend flour with sugar; using on/off motion, cut in butter until no visible pieces remain. Pour in egg; process until ball forms. Flatten into disc; wrap and refrigerate for 30 minutes. *(Pastry can be frozen for up to 2 months.)*

● On lightly floured surface, roll out pastry to 1/8-inch (3 mm) thickness; fit into 10-inch (25 cm) tart pan with removable bottom. Trim edge. Refrigerate for 1 hour or until chilled. *(Pastry shell can be wrapped and refrigerated for up to 3 days. Or freeze in rigid container for up to 2 months; bake frozen, adding 10 to 15 minutes to baking time.)*

● Prick bottom of pastry shell; line with foil and weigh down with pie weights or dried beans. Bake in 375°F (190°C) oven for 15 to 20 minutes or until dry. Remove weights and foil; bake for 15 to 20 minutes longer or just until golden brown. Let cool completely on rack. Makes 1 baked 10-inch (25 cm) tart shell, enough for 10 to 12 servings.

TIP: For a change, substitute whole wheat flour for the cake-and-pastry flour.

Lemon Hazelnut Tarts ▼

Both tarts and the lemon curd filling can be made ahead and frozen — ready to grace a dainty sweet tray at a moment's notice.

Per tart: about
• 80 calories   • 1 g protein
• 5 g fat   • 8 g carbohydrate

1/2 cup	hazelnuts	125 mL
1-1/2 cups	all-purpose flour	375 mL
1/4 cup	granulated sugar	50 mL
Pinch	salt	Pinch
1/2 cup	butter, cubed	125 mL
1	egg, beaten	1
1 tsp	vanilla	5 mL
	LEMON CURD	
3	egg yolks	3
2	eggs	2
3/4 cup	granulated sugar	175 mL
2 tsp	finely grated lemon rind	10 mL
2/3 cup	lemon juice	150 mL
1/3 cup	butter, cubed	75 mL

● Toast hazelnuts on baking sheet in 350°F (180°C) oven for 8 to 10 minutes or until fragrant. Place on clean tea towel; rub vigorously to remove most of the skins.

● Transfer nuts to food processor along with 1 tbsp (15 mL) of the flour; using on/off motion, chop just until fine. Blend in remaining flour, sugar and salt; using on/off motion, cut in butter until mixture resembles fine crumbs. Sprinkle with egg and vanilla; using on/off motion, blend until ball forms.

● Using about 2 tbsp (25 mL) dough per tart, press evenly into bottoms and up sides of 48 miniature (1-3/4-inch/4.5 cm) tart cups. Freeze for about 1 hour or until firm. *(Unbaked frozen shells can be removed from pans, layered between waxed paper in rigid airtight containers and frozen for up to 1 month. Return to pans before baking.)* Bake in 425°F (220°C) oven for 8 to 10 minutes or until golden. Let cool on rack.

● LEMON CURD: In heatproof bowl over simmering water, whisk together egg yolks, eggs, sugar, lemon rind and lemon juice; cook, whisking often, for about 12 minutes or until translucent and thickened to consistency of pudding. Remove from heat; add butter, stirring until melted. Pour into clean bowl; place plastic wrap directly on surface and refrigerate for about 1 hour or until chilled. *(Lemon curd can be refrigerated in airtight container for up to 1 week.)*

● Transfer shells to serving platter. Using piping bag or two spoons, fill each with 2 tsp (10 mL) of the lemon curd. *(Tarts can be covered and refrigerated for up to 4 hours.)* Makes 48 tarts.

TIPS

● You can also freeze baked tart shells, which is ideal if you're preparing large quantities for a party. Layer them between waxed paper in rigid airtight containers and freeze for up to 3 weeks; thaw at room temperature for 30 minutes.

● Or, to revive a fresh-baked flavor in frozen baked tart shells, warm on baking sheet in 350°F (180°C) oven for about 5 minutes or until fragrant. Let cool on racks before filling.

Plum and Almond Tart

2 cups	all-purpose flour	500 mL
1 tbsp	granulated sugar	15 mL
1/2 tsp	grated lemon rind	2 mL
1/4 tsp	salt	1 mL
3/4 cup	cold butter, cubed	175 mL
1	egg	1
1 tbsp	ice water	15 mL
	ALMOND FILLING	
1/3 cup	butter, softened	75 mL
1/2 cup	granulated sugar	125 mL
2	eggs	2
1/2 tsp	vanilla	2 mL
2/3 cup	ground almonds	150 mL
1-1/2 lb	prune plums, halved	750 g
	Icing sugar	

● In bowl, combine flour, sugar, lemon rind and salt; using pastry blender or two knives, cut in butter until mixture is in fine crumbs with a few larger pieces. Beat egg with water; drizzle over flour mixture, stirring briskly with fork until pastry holds together. Knead lightly into ball; flatten into disc. Wrap and refrigerate for 30 minutes. *(Pastry can be refrigerated for up to 3 days or frozen for up to 3 months; thaw if necessary. Let stand at room temperature for 15 minutes before rolling out.)*

● On lightly floured surface, roll out pastry to 1/8-inch (3 mm) thickness; fit into 11-inch (28 cm) flan pan with removable bottom. Refrigerate for 30 minutes. Prick pastry bottom with fork; line with foil and weigh down with pie weights or dried beans. Bake in 375°F (190°C) oven for 15 minutes. Remove weights and foil; bake for about 5 minutes longer or until golden. Let cool on rack.

● ALMOND FILLING: In bowl, beat butter with sugar; beat in eggs and vanilla. Stir in almonds until blended. Pour into cooled pastry shell. Decoratively arrange plums, cut side up, over filling.

● Bake in 350°F (180°C) oven for 30 to 40 minutes or until filling is golden brown and plums are tender. Let cool on rack. Sprinkle with icing sugar. Makes 10 servings.

Deep-purple prune plums create an eye-catching pattern when nestled in a cakelike almond filling.

Per serving: about
● 405 calories ● 6 g protein
● 25 g fat ● 40 g carbohydrate

Cranberry Pear Phyllo Tart ◀

9	sheets phyllo pastry	9
1/2 cup	butter, melted	125 mL
1/3 cup	granulated sugar	75 mL
	FILLING	
3 cups	cranberries (fresh or frozen), 12 oz (375 g)	750 mL
4	pears (Bartlett or Anjou), peeled, cored and diced	4
1 cup	golden raisins	250 mL
1 cup	granulated sugar	250 mL
1/2 cup	orange juice	125 mL
1 tbsp	cornstarch	15 mL
1 tbsp	grated orange rind	15 mL
	GARNISH	
	Phyllo Flowers and Frosted Cranberries (see Finishing Touches, below)	
1 tbsp	grated orange rind	15 mL
	Mint sprigs (optional)	

● FILLING: Set aside 1/4 cup (50 mL) of the cranberries for garnish. In saucepan, combine remaining cranberries, pears, raisins, sugar and orange juice; bring to boil. Reduce heat to medium; cover and cook, stirring occasionally, for about 8 minutes or until pears are almost tender and cranberries pop.

● Combine cornstarch with 1 tbsp (15 mL) cold water and stir into fruit mixture; cook for about 1 minute or until thickened. Remove from heat; stir in orange rind. Let cool.

● Arrange 1 sheet of the phyllo on work surface, keeping remaining phyllo covered with damp towel to prevent drying out. Brush lightly with butter. Place in lightly greased 10-inch (25 cm) tart pan with removable bottom, letting excess hang over edge. Sprinkle with 2 tsp (10 mL) of the sugar.

● Brush second sheet with butter; place on first, rotating a quarter turn. Sprinkle with another 2 tsp (10 mL) sugar. Layer with 2 more sheets, brushing each with butter, sprinkling with sugar and rotating so phyllo is not aligned with layers below.

● Gently press down phyllo to fit pan. Spread with filling; one at a time, fold phyllo edges over top. One at a time, place remaining phyllo on top of pie, rotating, buttering and sprinkling each with sugar. Gently fold top phyllo layers under tart. Using knife, cut steam vents in top. *(Tart can be prepared to this point, covered loosely with plastic wrap and refrigerated for up to 4 hours.)*

● Bake in 400°F (200°C) oven for 30 to 35 minutes or until pastry is crisp and golden. Remove from oven; let stand for 10 minutes in pan on rack. Remove from pan; slide onto large serving platter.

● GARNISH: Top with phyllo flowers. Scatter frosted cranberries on top and around side. Top with orange rind, and mint (if using). Serve warm. Makes 12 servings.

This phyllo tart, plumped with ruby-red cranberries and crowned with sugar-dusted phyllo flowers, is a dessert dazzler, ideal for entertaining. Take the kudos, but don't let on how easy it is to make.

Per serving: about
- 315 calories
- 3 g protein
- 9 g fat
- 61 g carbohydrate

FINISHING TOUCHES

Phyllo Flowers
● Arrange 2 stacked sheets of phyllo pastry on work surface. Using knife, trace six 4-inch (10 cm) circles; cut out. Wet center of 1 circle with water; top with second circle. Pinch centers together to make flower shape. Spray with nonstick cooking spray; place in small muffin cups. Sprinkle with 1/4 tsp (1 mL) granulated sugar. Repeat with remaining circles. Bake in 400°F (200°C) oven for 8 to 10 minutes or until golden. Let cool.

Frosted Cranberries
● In bowl, lightly beat 1 egg white until frothy. Pour 1/4 cup (50 mL) granulated sugar into shallow bowl. Dip reserved cranberries, a few at a time, in egg white; remove with slotted spoon. Roll in sugar until coated. Place on paper towel-lined rack; let dry for 1 hour.

Fruit Plus Flour

Fresh from the oven or hot from the griddle come easy-to-make golden brown muffins, crusty scones, delectable breads and a stack of pancakes — all fragrant and plumped with a tumble of fruit.

Banana Lemon Loaves ▶

Banana loaf is delicious on its own, and even better with lemon highlights.

Per slice: about
- 310 calories
- 10 g fat
- 6 g protein
- 49 g carbohydrate

3 cups	mashed ripe bananas (about 6)	750 mL
2 tbsp	grated lemon rind	25 mL
1/2 cup	lemon juice	125 mL
1/3 cup	butter, softened	75 mL
1/3 cup	shortening	75 mL
1 cup	granulated sugar	250 mL
4	eggs	4
2 tsp	vanilla	10 mL
3-3/4 cups	all-purpose flour	925 mL
2 tsp	baking soda	10 mL
1-1/2 tsp	baking powder	7 mL
1-1/2 tsp	grated nutmeg	7 mL
3/4 tsp	salt	4 mL

● Combine bananas with lemon rind and juice; set aside.

● In large bowl, beat together butter, shortening and sugar until light and fluffy; beat in eggs, one at a time. Stir in banana mixture and vanilla.

● Stir together flour, baking soda, baking powder, nutmeg and salt; stir into batter one-third at a time.

● Spoon into 5 greased 5-3/4- x 3-1/4-inch (500 mL) foil pans. Bake in 350°F (180°C) oven for about 40 minutes or until golden and cake tester inserted in center comes out clean.

● Let cool in pans on racks for 15 minutes. Remove from pans; let cool completely on racks. *(Loaves can be wrapped in plastic wrap and stored in airtight container for up to 3 days or frozen in rigid airtight container.)* Makes 5 small loaves, 3 slices each.

TIP: If you have a kitchen scale, you can divide the batter evenly in pans by weight — each filled pan should weigh about 11-1/2 oz (330 g).

BAKING WITH BANANAS

Ripe yellow bananas, freckled and fragrant, make all the difference in these loaves. Plan ahead to let bananas ripen for a few days at room temperature. For faster ripening, place bananas in a bag.

Pumpkin Loaves

Mini loaves that mix the spiciness of gingerbread with the moist richness of pumpkin are ideal for small households or for gift giving.

Per loaf: about
- 425 calories
- 6 g protein
- 15 g fat
- 67 g carbohydrate
- good source of iron

2/3 cup	butter, softened	150 mL
2/3 cup	packed brown sugar	150 mL
2	eggs	2
1/3 cup	fancy molasses	75 mL
2-3/4 cups	all-purpose flour	675 mL
2 tsp	ground ginger	10 mL
1 tsp	each baking soda, baking powder and cinnamon	5 mL
1/2 tsp	grated nutmeg	2 mL
Pinch	each allspice, salt and pepper	Pinch
1	can (14 oz/398 mL) pumpkin purée	1
1/3 cup	buttermilk	75 mL
3/4 cup	icing sugar, sifted	175 mL
1 tbsp	orange juice	15 mL

● In bowl, beat butter with brown sugar until fluffy. Beat in eggs, one at a time; beat in molasses.

● Stir together flour, ginger, baking soda, baking powder, cinnamon, nutmeg, allspice, salt and pepper; stir one-third into butter mixture. Stir in pumpkin. Stir in another third of the flour mixture; stir in buttermilk. Stir in remaining flour mixture.

● Scrape into 9 greased 3-1/2- x 2-1/2-inch (125 mL) mini loaf pans or 9-inch (2.5 L) square cake pan. Bake in 350°F (180°C) oven for about 30 minutes for mini loaves, 45 minutes for cake or until cake tester inserted in center comes out clean. Let cool in pans on racks for 20 minutes; turn out onto racks and let cool completely.

● Stir icing sugar with orange juice; drizzle over loaves. Makes 9 mini loaves.

Orange Prune Sour Cream Loaf

What's nice about loaves is that you don't have to be an experienced baker to produce a perfect specimen!

Per slice: about
- 275 calories
- 4 g protein
- 12 g fat
- 40 g carbohydrate

1/2 cup	butter, softened	125 mL
1 cup	granulated sugar	250 mL
2	eggs	2
2 cups	all-purpose flour	500 mL
1 tsp	baking powder	5 mL
1/2 tsp	baking soda	2 mL
1/2 tsp	salt	2 mL
1/2 cup	quartered pitted prunes	125 mL
2 tbsp	coarsely grated orange rind	25 mL
1 cup	sour cream	250 mL
	GLAZE	
2 tbsp	granulated sugar	25 mL
2 tbsp	orange juice	25 mL

● Grease 9- x 5-inch (2 L) loaf pan; line bottom with waxed paper; set aside.

● In bowl, beat butter with sugar until light and fluffy; beat in eggs, one at a time. Stir together flour, baking powder, baking soda and salt; remove about 2/3 cup (150 mL) and toss with quartered prunes and orange rind. Set aside.

● Mix half of the remaining dry ingredients into butter mixture, then half of the sour cream; repeat additions. Sprinkle with prune mixture; stir just until blended.

● Scrape into prepared pan; bake in 350°F (180°C) oven for 55 to 60 minutes or until cake tester inserted in center comes out clean. Let cool in pan on rack for 10 minutes; invert onto rack and peel off paper. Turn right side up.

● GLAZE: Stir sugar with orange juice until dissolved; brush over warm loaf. Let cool completely. *(Loaf can be wrapped in plastic wrap and stored in refrigerator for up to 3 days or frozen in rigid airtight container for up to 1 week.)* Makes 12 slices.

Strawberry Tea Bread

3 cups	strawberries, coarsely chopped	750 mL
1 cup	chopped almonds	250 mL
3-1/2 cups	all-purpose flour	875 mL
1 cup	butter, softened	250 mL
1-1/2 cups	granulated sugar	375 mL
3	eggs	3
1/2 tsp	almond extract	2 mL
2 tsp	baking powder	10 mL
3/4 tsp	each baking soda and salt	4 mL
1/2 tsp	cinnamon	2 mL
1/4 tsp	grated nutmeg	1 mL
3/4 cup	buttermilk	175 mL

● In bowl, gently toss together strawberries, almonds and 1/4 cup (50 mL) of the flour; set aside.

● In large bowl, beat butter with sugar until light and fluffy; beat in eggs, one at a time. Beat in almond extract.

● Stir together remaining flour, baking powder, baking soda, salt, cinnamon and nutmeg; stir into flour mixture alternately with buttermilk, making three additions of flour mixture and two of buttermilk. Gently fold in strawberry mixture.

● Spoon into 2 greased and floured 8- x 4-inch (1.5 L) loaf pans. Bake in 350°F (180°C) oven for about 1 hour or until cake tester inserted in center comes out clean. Let cool in pans on racks for 10 minutes. Remove from pans; let cool completely on racks. (*Bread can be wrapped in plastic wrap and stored for up to 1 day or frozen in rigid airtight container for up to 2 weeks.*) Makes 2 loaves, 16 slices each.

Y*ou'll find a berry in almost every bite. That's a promise!*

Per slice: about
- 175 calories
- 9 g fat
- 3 g protein
- 22 g carbohydrate

Raspberry Pinwheel Biscuits

1/2 cup	raspberry jam	125 mL
1-1/4 tsp	cinnamon	6 mL
2 cups	all-purpose flour	500 mL
1 tbsp	each granulated sugar and baking powder	15 mL
1/2 tsp	salt	2 mL
1/3 cup	shortening	75 mL
3/4 cup	buttermilk	175 mL
1 tsp	vanilla	5 mL
2 tbsp	butter, softened	25 mL
1/2 cup	icing sugar, sifted	125 mL
1 tbsp	milk	15 mL

● Stir raspberry jam with cinnamon; set aside. In large bowl, stir together flour, sugar, baking powder and salt; using pastry blender or two knives, cut in shortening until crumbly. Add buttermilk and vanilla; stir with fork to make soft, sticky dough.

● Turn out onto lightly floured surface; knead about 10 times or until smooth. Keeping surface floured, roll out to 16- x 10-inch (40 x 25 cm) rectangle; spread with butter then raspberry jam mixture, leaving 1-inch (2.5 cm) border along one long edge. Starting at opposite long edge, roll up dough jelly roll-style; pinch seam to seal. Cut into 12 slices.

● Place slices, cut side down, in greased 9-inch (1.5 L) round cake pan. (*Pan can be wrapped in plastic wrap and frozen in rigid airtight container for up to 2 weeks. Let thaw in refrigerator for about 12 hours; add 5 minutes to baking time.*) Bake in 425°F (220°C) oven for about 30 minutes or until browned. Let cool slightly.

● In bowl, whisk icing sugar with milk until smooth. Drizzle over biscuits. Serve warm. Make 12 biscuits.

W*ith these biscuits in the freezer, ready to pop into the oven for brunch or breakfast, you can count on just-baked goodness in a relaxed style.*

Per biscuit: about
- 210 calories
- 8 g fat
- 3 g protein
- 32 g carbohydrate

Braided Raspberry Danish Wreath ◄

1/3 cup	granulated sugar	75 mL
1/4 cup	warm water	50 mL
2 tsp	quick-rising (instant) dry yeast	10 mL
2-1/2 cups	all-purpose flour (approx)	625 mL
3/4 tsp	salt	4 mL
1/2 tsp	cardamom or cinnamon	2 mL
1/2 cup	cold butter, cubed	125 mL
1/4 cup	milk	50 mL
1	egg	1
1/4 cup	sliced almonds	50 mL
1/4 cup	raspberry jam	50 mL
	GLAZE	
1	egg yolk	1
1 tbsp	water	15 mL
	ICING	
1/2 cup	sifted icing sugar	125 mL
4 tsp	milk	20 mL
1 tbsp	butter, melted	15 mL

● In small bowl, dissolve a pinch of the sugar in warm water. Sprinkle in yeast; let stand for 10 minutes or until frothy.

● In large bowl, stir together remaining sugar, flour, salt and cardamom; using pastry blender or two knives, cut in butter until mixture is in fine crumbs. With electric mixer, beat in yeast mixture, milk and egg until soft sticky dough forms and begins to pull away from side of bowl.

● Turn out onto lightly floured surface; knead lightly for 5 minutes, adding only as much more flour as necessary to prevent excessive sticking. (Dough should be soft and slightly sticky.) Place in greased bowl, turning to grease all over. *(Dough can be covered and refrigerated overnight; omit the next rise and shape into wreath directly from refrigerator.)* Cover with plastic wrap; let rise in warm, draft-free spot until doubled in bulk, 1 to 1-1/2 hours. Deflate dough gently with fingertips; refrigerate for 2 hours.

● Turn out dough onto lightly floured surface; roll out to 14-inch (35 cm) circle. Fold in half; transfer to large piece of lightly greased foil and unfold. Using 3-inch (8 cm) round cookie cutter, mark (but do not cut) circle in center of dough. Starting at edge and ending about 1 inch (2.5 cm) outside marked circle, cut dough evenly into 24 strips.

● Braid 3 of the strips together; pinch ends to join. Repeat with remaining strips to form 8 braids. Curl each braid in same direction, pressing end to beginning of braid. Slide foil onto 12-inch (30 cm) or larger round pizza pan. Trim or fold down excess foil. With 3-inch (8 cm) round cookie cutter, cut out hole from center circle of dough. Cover with tea towel; let rise for 40 minutes or until almost doubled in bulk and dough does not spring back quickly when lightly pressed. Meanwhile, place almonds in freezer and jam in refrigerator.

● GLAZE: Whisk egg yolk with water; brush over wreath. With fingertips or back of spoon, press 1-inch (2.5 cm) indentation into center of each curled braid; fill with 1-1/2 tsp (7 mL) jam. Sprinkle almonds around center hole, pressing lightly to adhere. Bake in 350°F (180°C) oven for 25 to 30 minutes or until golden brown. *(Wreath can be prepared to this point, cooled, wrapped in plastic wrap and frozen in rigid airtight container for up to 2 weeks. Reheat frozen, unwrapped wreath in 350°F/180°C oven for 15 to 20 minutes or until warmed through.)*

● ICING: In small bowl, whisk together sugar, milk and butter; drizzle over hot wreath. Transfer to serving plate. Serve warm or at room temperature. *(Danish can be stored in airtight container for up to 1 day.)* Makes 8 servings.

When the occasion calls for something spectacular, try this beautiful (freezeable!) wreath.

Per serving: about
- 385 calories
- 17 g fat
- good source of iron
- 7 g protein
- 53 g carbohydrate

Cherry Kuchen

This kuchen — with a judiciously sweetened bread layer as its base, a generous sprinkle of tart cherries and a tastefully balanced streusel topping — is the original yeast-raised kind. It's just right for a brunch or for afternoon tea.

Per serving: about
- 260 calories
- 5 g protein
- 8 g fat
- 40 g carbohydrate

1/4 cup	granulated sugar	50 mL
1 cup	warm water	250 mL
2 tsp	active dry yeast	10 mL
2 tbsp	butter, melted	25 mL
1 tbsp	grated lemon rind	15 mL
1 tsp	salt	5 mL
3/4 tsp	almond extract	4 mL
3 cups	all-purpose flour (approx)	750 mL
1/2 cup	ground almonds	125 mL
2 cups	drained canned cherries or thawed sour cherries	500 mL
	STREUSEL	
1/2 cup	all-purpose flour	125 mL
1/4 cup	packed brown sugar	50 mL
1/4 cup	butter, softened	50 mL

● In large bowl, dissolve 1 tsp (5 mL) of the sugar in warm water. Sprinkle in yeast; let stand for about 10 minutes or until frothy.

● Whisk in remaining sugar, butter, lemon rind, salt and almond extract. Whisk in 1 cup (50 mL) of the flour; with wooden spoon, beat in enough of the remaining flour to make stiff but sticky dough.

● Turn out dough onto lightly floured surface; knead for 5 minutes or until smooth and elastic. Place in greased bowl, turning to grease all over. Cover with plastic wrap; let rise in warm draft-free place until doubled in bulk, 1 to 1-1/2 hours.

● Punch down dough; stretch onto greased 15- x 10-inch (40 x 25 cm) jelly roll pan. Sprinkle evenly with ground almonds, then cherries.

● STREUSEL: In small bowl, combine flour with sugar; with pastry blender or fork, cut in butter until crumbly. Sprinkle over cherries.

● Cover with plastic wrap; let rise for 20 minutes. Bake in 400°F (200°C) oven for 15 to 20 minutes or until bottom is golden. Let cool in pan on rack. *(Kuchen can be wrapped in plastic wrap and frozen in rigid airtight container for up to 1 week.)* Makes 12 servings.

VARIATION

● BREAD MACHINE CHERRY KUCHEN (for dough only): In order, place in pan: water, sugar, butter, lemon rind, almond extract, salt, flour and 2 tsp (10 mL) quick-rising active dry yeast. (Do not let yeast touch liquids.) Choose dough setting. Remove from machine; shape and bake as directed.

Clementine Poppy Seed Muffins

2-1/4 cups	all-purpose flour	550 mL
1/2 cup	granulated sugar	125 mL
1/4 cup	poppy seeds	50 mL
1 tbsp	baking powder	15 mL
1 tsp	ground ginger	5 mL
3/4 tsp	baking soda	4 mL
3	clementines	3
1 cup	low-fat plain yogurt	250 mL
2	eggs	2
1/4 cup	butter, melted	50 mL

● In bowl, stir together flour, sugar, poppy seeds, baking powder, ginger and baking soda. Finely grate rind of 2 of the clementines; add to bowl.

● Peel all clementines and coarsely chop segments to make about 1 cup (250 mL); add to flour mixture and toss to coat. Whisk together yogurt, eggs and butter. Pour over flour mixture; stir just until moistened.

● Spoon into 10 greased or paper-lined muffin cups, filling two-thirds full. Bake in 375°F (190°C) oven for 20 to 25 minutes or until golden and tops are firm to the touch. Let cool in pan on rack for 5 minutes; transfer to rack and let cool completely. *(Muffins can be individually wrapped in plastic wrap and refrigerated for up to 2 days or frozen in airtight container for up to 3 weeks.)* Makes 10 muffins.

Either clementines or mandarins are right for this appealing wintertime muffin.

Per muffin: about
- 245 calories
- 6 g protein
- 8 g fat
- 38 g carbohydrate

Orange Banana Muffins

2 cups	whole wheat flour	500 mL
1/3 cup	natural bran	75 mL
1 tsp	baking powder	5 mL
1 tsp	baking soda	5 mL
1/4 tsp	salt	1 mL
1 cup	mashed banana	250 mL
1/2 cup	frozen orange juice concentrate, thawed	125 mL
1/4 cup	packed brown sugar	50 mL
1/4 cup	vegetable oil	50 mL
1/4 cup	milk	50 mL
1	egg	1
1 tsp	grated orange rind	5 mL

● In large bowl, stir together whole wheat flour, natural bran, baking powder, baking soda and salt.

● Whisk together banana, orange juice concentrate, brown sugar, oil, milk, egg and orange rind. Pour over dry ingredients; stir just until moistened.

● Spoon into greased or paper-lined muffin cups, filling to top. Bake in 400°F (200°C) oven for 20 to 25 minutes or until tops are firm to the touch. Let cool in pan on rack for 5 minutes; transfer to rack and let cool completely. Makes 12 small or 8 medium muffins.

Guaranteed not to crumble in the car or on the school bus, this is the perfect muffin for breakfast on the run or for after-school snacks. Need we add that it's also chock-full of goodness, and freezeable, too?

Per small muffin: about
- 175 calories
- 4 g protein
- 6 g fat
- 29 g carbohydrate

TIP: To freeze muffins, wrap each one in plastic wrap, then enclose the batch in an airtight container or freezer bag. This double protection prevents them from drying out.

Blueberry Oat Bran Muffins

Getting enough fiber in your diet is so much easier when you start off the day with these delicious, high-fiber muffins.

Per muffin: about
- 180 calories
- 7 g protein
- 6 g fat
- 29 g carbohydrate
- high source of fiber

1 cup	whole wheat flour	250 mL
1 cup	oat bran	250 mL
3/4 cup	wheat germ	175 mL
1/2 cup	packed brown sugar	125 mL
1 tbsp	grated lemon rind	15 mL
2 tsp	baking powder	10 mL
1 tsp	baking soda	5 mL
1/4 tsp	salt	1 mL
2	eggs	2
1-1/2 cups	buttermilk	375 mL
3 tbsp	vegetable oil	50 mL
1-1/2 cups	blueberries	375 mL

● In large bowl, stir together whole wheat flour, oat bran, wheat germ, brown sugar, lemon rind, baking powder, baking soda and salt.

● In separate bowl, lightly beat eggs; stir in buttermilk and oil. Pour over dry ingredients; sprinkle with blueberries. Stir just until dry ingredients are moistened.

● Spoon into 12 greased or paper-lined muffin cups. Bake in 400°F (200°C) oven for 20 minutes or until tops are firm to the touch. Let cool in pan on rack for 5 minutes; transfer to rack and let cool completely. Makes 12 muffins.

Banana Buttermilk Pancakes

When making pancakes for a weekend breakfast, wrap any leftovers in plastic wrap and enclose in a freezer bag to freeze for a busy morning when you only have time to pop a pancake or two into the toaster.

Per pancake: about
- 110 calories
- 3 g protein
- 4 g fat
- 15 g carbohydrate

3/4 cup	all-purpose flour	175 mL
3/4 cup	whole wheat flour	175 mL
2 tbsp	granulated sugar	25 mL
1 tsp	baking soda	5 mL
1/2 tsp	cinnamon	2 mL
1/4 tsp	salt	1 mL
2 cups	buttermilk	500 mL
1 cup	mashed bananas	250 mL
1/4 cup	butter, melted	50 mL
2	eggs	2
	Vegetable oil for skillet	

● In large bowl, stir together all-purpose and whole wheat flours, sugar, baking soda, cinnamon and salt. Whisk together buttermilk, bananas, butter and eggs; pour over dry ingredients and stir just until moistened.

● Heat skillet or griddle over medium heat; brush with oil. Using 1/4 cup (50 mL) batter for each pancake, pour into skillet; cook for about 2 minutes or until bottom is golden and bubbles break on top but do not fill in. Turn and cook for about 1 minute or until bottom is golden. Makes 16 pancakes.

Peachy Pancakes

1 cup	all-purpose flour	250 mL
1/2 cup	whole wheat flour	125 mL
3 tbsp	granulated sugar	50 mL
1 tsp	baking soda	5 mL
1/4 tsp	each grated nutmeg and salt	1 mL
1 cup	plain yogurt	250 mL
3/4 cup	milk	175 mL
2 tbsp	butter, melted	25 mL
2	eggs	2
	Vegetable oil for skillet	
1-1/4 cups	finely chopped peeled peaches	300 mL

● In large bowl, stir together all-purpose and whole wheat flours, sugar, baking soda, nutmeg and salt. Whisk together yogurt, milk, butter and eggs; pour over dry ingredients and stir just until moistened.

● Heat skillet or griddle over medium heat; brush with oil. Using 1/4 cup (50 mL) batter for each pancake, pour into skillet; sprinkle 1 tbsp (15 mL) peaches over each. Cook for about 2 minutes or until bottom is golden and bubbles break on top but do not fill in. Turn and cook for about 2 minutes or until bottom is golden. Makes 16 pancakes.

*B*reakfast is a treat with golden, light and healthy pancakes studded with chunks of glorious fresh peaches.

Per pancake: about
- 95 calories
- 3 g fat
- 3 g protein
- 14 g carbohydrate

Blueberry Lemon Blintzes

1	egg	1
1	egg yolk	1
1/4 tsp	salt	1 mL
2/3 cup	all-purpose flour	150 mL
4 tsp	butter	20 mL
	FILLING	
1 cup	pressed cottage cheese (8 oz/250 g)	250 mL
1	egg yolk	1
2 tbsp	granulated sugar	25 mL
1 tsp	all-purpose flour	5 mL
1/2 cup	blueberries (fresh or frozen)	125 mL
1/2 tsp	grated lemon rind	2 mL

● In blender or bowl, beat together egg, egg yolk, salt and 3/4 cup (175 mL) water. Blend in flour until smooth; transfer to bowl. Cover with plastic wrap and refrigerate for at least 1 hour or for up to 4 hours.

● Melt 2 tsp (10 mL) of the butter. Heat 7-inch (18 cm) crêpe pan over medium-high heat; brush lightly with some of the melted butter. Stir batter; pour 3 tbsp (50 mL) into pan, tilting to spread. Cook for 45 to 60 seconds or until set and no longer moist in center. Invert onto tea towel. Repeat with remaining butter and batter, placing waxed paper between each cooked blintz.

● FILLING: In bowl, beat cottage cheese until fluffy; beat in egg yolk, sugar and flour. Gently fold in blueberries and lemon rind. Spoon heaping tbsp (15 mL) along center of 1 blintz. Fold 1 edge over filling; fold opposite edge over, then ends, to form envelope. Repeat with remaining filling and blintzes. *(Blintzes can be prepared to this point, wrapped individually in plastic wrap and frozen in rigid airtight container for up to 2 weeks.)*

● In nonstick skillet, melt remaining butter over medium heat; cook blintzes for 2 minutes per side or until warmed through. (Alternatively, cook frozen blintzes for 4 minutes per side or toast in 425°F/220°C toaster oven for 15 minutes.) Makes 8 blintzes, or 4 servings.

*B*lintzes, unlike crêpes, are cooked on one side only. These freezeable blintzes feature the traditional filling of pressed cottage cheese dolled up with lemon rind and blueberries.

Per serving: about
- 245 calories
- 8 g fat
- 15 g protein
- 27 g carbohydrate

Summer in a Jar

Here's how to preserve a little summer, with our best-ever jams, jellies and relishes. We've included family-favorite recipes plus tasty new sweet-and-savory combos that are sure to please — especially when summer is a winter's dream away!

Rumtopf Revival ▶

A bounty of summer's best berries and fruit slumber and mellow in rum and sugar until the end of the year. This is heaven over ice cream.

Per 1/2 cup (125 mL): about
- 205 calories
- 1 g protein
- trace fat
- 52 g carbohydrate

3 cups	small strawberries (1 lb/500 g)	750 mL
6-3/4 cups	granulated sugar	1.675 L
1	bottle (1 L) amber rum	1
3-1/2 cups	raspberries or blackberries (1 lb/500 g)	875 mL
4 cups	sweet cherries, pierced several times (1 lb/500 g)	1 L
2-1/4 cups	blueberries (1 lb/500 g)	675 mL
3 cups	sliced pitted plums (1 lb/500 g whole)	750 mL
2 cups	sliced pitted peaches (1-1/2 lb/750 g whole)	500 mL

● In sterilized wide-mouthed 16-cup (4 L) jar with tight-fitting lid, stir strawberries with 1 cup (250 mL) plus 2 tbsp (25 mL) of the sugar; let stand for 30 minutes. Slowly pour in rum, without stirring. Cover and store in refrigerator, stirring after a few days to dissolve sugar.

● Allowing 2 weeks between additions, add fruit as follows: in bowl, stir raspberries with 1 cup (250 mL) plus 2 tbsp (25 mL) of the sugar; let stand for 30 minutes. Stir into strawberries. Cover and store in refrigerator, stirring after a few days to dissolve sugar.

● Repeat with cherries, blueberries, plums and peaches. Makes about 16 cups (4 L).

PRESERVING BASICS

● Fill boiling water-bath canner two-thirds full of water. About 30 minutes before filling jars, start to boil.

● Use only new lids and canning jars free of nicks and cracks.

● Wash, rinse and air-dry jars. Fifteen minutes before filling, place jars, funnel and 1/2 cup (125 mL) metal measure in canner rack; boil for 15 minutes.

● Boil new canning lids with jars for last 5 minutes.

● Fill jars, using funnel and metal measure for ladling, leaving recommended headspace. Avoid splashing onto rim of jar; wipe rim, if necessary.

● Center lids on jars; screw on bands until fingertip-tight.

● Return jars to canner. If necessary, add enough boiling water to cover jars by at least 1 inch (2.5 cm). Cover and return to boil; boil for specified time.

● Let jars cool on rack for 24 hours. Check that lids curve downward. (If any don't, refrigerate and use within 3 weeks.) Label and store in cool, dry, dark place for up to 1 year.

Apricot Ginger Chutney ▼

Truly gingery, and studded with soothing apricots and apples, this chutney is adapted from a recipe by Madhur Jaffrey, Indian-cooking TV personality, teacher and author.

Per tbsp (15 mL): about
- 50 calories
- trace protein
- trace fat
- 12 g carbohydrate

6 cups	coarsely chopped peeled apples	1.5 L
4 cups	packed dried apricots, halved (1-3/4 lb/875 g)	1 L
3 cups	white wine vinegar	750 mL
1 cup	golden raisins	250 mL
1/2 cup	grated gingerroot	125 mL
8	cloves garlic, slivered	8
1/2 tsp	salt	2 mL
1/4 tsp	hot pepper flakes	1 mL
4 cups	granulated sugar	1 L

● In large heavy nonaluminum pot, combine apples, apricots, vinegar, raisins, ginger, garlic, salt and hot pepper flakes; bring to boil. Cover and reduce heat to low; simmer for 10 minutes or until apricots are plumped.

● Stir in sugar and return to simmer; cook, stirring almost constantly, for 20 minutes or until thickened.

● Remove from heat. Pour into eight 1-cup (250 mL) canning jars, leaving 1/2-inch (1 cm) headspace. Seal with prepared discs and bands. Process in boiling water bath for 10 minutes. (See Preserving Basics, p. 76.) Let cool. Makes 8 cups (2 L).

Peach and Raisin Chutney ▼

Chutneys add the spice of life to cold meats, and their sweet and sour edges are rounded off nicely with cheese, especially a cream cheese or a buttery Jarlsberg.

Per tbsp (15 mL): about
- 30 calories
- trace protein
- 0 g fat
- 7 g carbohydrate

8 cups	sliced peeled peaches (3-1/2 lb/1.75 kg)	2 L
2 cups	packed brown sugar	500 mL
2 cups	chopped onions	500 mL
2 cups	raisins	500 mL
2 cups	cider vinegar	500 mL
1/2 cup	diced sweet red pepper	125 mL
2 tsp	mustard seeds	10 mL
1 tsp	salt	5 mL
1/2 tsp	each turmeric, cinnamon, curry powder, ground cumin and coriander	2 mL
Pinch	cayenne pepper	Pinch

● In large heavy nonaluminum pot, combine peaches, sugar, onions, raisins, vinegar, red pepper, mustard seeds, salt, turmeric, cinnamon, curry powder, cumin, coriander and cayenne; bring to boil. Reduce heat to medium; simmer, stirring often, for 1 hour or until thickened and toffee-brown in color.

● Remove from heat. Pour into eight 1-cup (250 mL) canning jars, leaving 1/2-inch (1 cm) headspace. Seal with prepared discs and bands. Process in boiling water bath for 10 minutes. (See Preserving Basics, p. 76.) Let cool. Makes 8 cups (2 L).

Apple Mint Chutney ▼

2	large lemons	2
6 cups	chopped peeled apples	1.5 L
6 cups	chopped onions	1.5 L
3 cups	diced peeled tomatoes	750 mL
2-1/2 cups	granulated sugar	625 mL
2 cups	cider vinegar	500 mL
1-1/2 cups	raisins	375 mL
2/3 cup	lightly packed chopped fresh mint (or 2 tbsp/25 mL dried)	150 mL
1/4 cup	chopped fresh parsley	50 mL
1/2 tsp	each salt and cinnamon	2 mL
Pinch	cayenne pepper	Pinch

● With zester, remove rind from lemons. (Or pare off thin outer rind and cut into thin strips.) Squeeze and strain juice into large heavy nonaluminum pot.

● Stir in lemon rind, apples, onions, tomatoes, sugar, vinegar, raisins, mint, parsley, salt, cinnamon and cayenne; bring to boil. Reduce heat to low; simmer for 1-1/2 hours or until thickened.

● Remove from heat. Pour into eight 1-cup (250 mL) canning jars, leaving 1/2-inch (1 cm) headspace. Seal with prepared discs and bands. Process in boiling water bath for 10 minutes. (See Preserving Basics, p. 76.) Let cool. Makes 12 cups (3 L).

Some chutneys benefit from a bit of mellowing before sampling, but this mint-flecked delight is blended well enough to enjoy right away.

Per tbsp (15 mL): about
- 20 calories
- trace protein
- 0 g fat
- 5 g carbohydrate

Ruby Beet and Apple Chutney ▼

8	large beets (2 lb/1 kg)	8
1	lemon	1
3 cups	chopped peeled apples	750 mL
2 cups	granulated sugar	500 mL
2 cups	chopped onions	500 mL
2 cups	cider vinegar	500 mL
1/2 cup	raisins	125 mL
1/4 cup	diced candied ginger	50 mL
1 tsp	mustard seeds	5 mL
1/2 tsp	each salt and pepper	2 mL

● Trim beets, leaving tails intact and 1 inch (2.5 cm) of stems. In saucepan of boiling water, cook beets for 30 minutes or until skins can be slipped off easily; drain and let cool. Slip off skins; dice to make 4-1/2 cups (1.125 L).

● Meanwhile, with zester, remove rind from lemon. (Or pare off thin outer rind and cut into thin strips.) Squeeze and strain juice into large heavy nonaluminum saucepan.

● Stir in lemon rind, apples, sugar, onions, vinegar, raisins, ginger, mustard seeds, salt and pepper; bring to boil. Reduce heat to low; simmer, stirring often, for 30 minutes or until apples are tender. Stir in beets; cook for 10 to 15 minutes or until thickened.

● Remove from heat. Pour into six 1-cup (250 mL) canning jars, leaving 1/2-inch (1 cm) headspace. Seal with prepared discs and bands. Process in boiling water bath for 10 minutes. (See Preserving Basics, p. 76.) Let cool. Make 6 cups (1.5 L).

Beets are a novel but beautiful ingredient in chutney. Their sweetness marries deliciously with apples and helps counter the acidic thrust of the vinegar.

Per tbsp (15 mL): about
- 30 calories
- trace protein
- 0 g fat
- 7 g carbohydrate

Fruit Chili Sauce

A *traditional tomato chili sauce was adapted to take advantage of the wealth of fruit available at the end of summer.*

Per tbsp (15 mL): about
- 20 calories
- trace protein
- trace fat
- 5 g carbohydrate

8 cups	chopped peeled tomatoes (3 lb/1.5 kg)	2 L
3 cups	chopped peeled pears	750 mL
3 cups	chopped sweet red peppers	750 mL
2-1/2 cups	chopped peeled peaches	625 mL
2-1/2 cups	chopped peeled apples	625 mL
2-1/2 cups	chopped onions	625 mL
2-1/4 cups	packed brown sugar	550 mL
2-1/4 cups	cider vinegar	550 mL
4 tsp	salt	20 mL
1/2 tsp	cinnamon	2 mL
2 tbsp	pickling spice	25 mL

● In large heavy nonaluminum pot, stir together tomatoes, pears, red peppers, peaches, apples, onions, brown sugar, vinegar, salt and cinnamon. Tie pickling spice in double thickness cheesecloth bag; add to pan. Bring to boil, stirring often. Reduce heat to medium; boil gently, stirring frequently, for 1-1/2 to 2 hours or until very thick. Discard spice bag.

● Remove from heat. Pour into five 2-cup (500 mL) canning jars, leaving 1/2-inch (1 cm) headspace. Seal with prepared discs and bands. Process in boiling water bath for 20 minutes. (See Preserving Basics, p. 76.) Let cool. Makes about 10 cups (2.5 L).

Five-Spice Pears

I*t's worth searching out star anise and cardamom to make these sensational dessert pears created by chef Kate Gammal. Chinese groceries have star anise; Indian groceries stock green cardamom (the best kind).*

Per serving of pear half plus 2 tbsp (25 mL) liquid: about
- 140 calories
- trace protein
- trace fat
- 35 g carbohydrate

1/2 cup	lemon juice	125 mL
4 lb	small pears (12 to 14)	2 kg
3 cups	granulated sugar	750 mL
1-1/2 cups	dry red wine	375 mL
2	strips lemon rind (2- x 1-inch/5 x 2.5 cm)	2
4	slices gingerroot	4
2	sticks cinnamon , halved	2
4	whole star anise	4
1/2 tsp	each whole cloves and cardamom	2 mL
1/4 tsp	black peppercorns	1 mL

● In large bowl, combine half of the lemon juice and 6 cups (1.5 L) water. Peel, halve and core pears, adding to bowl as you work. Let stand for no longer than 20 minutes.

● Meanwhile, in large heavy nonaluminum saucepan, dissolve sugar in remaining lemon juice, wine and 3 cups (750 mL) water. Add lemon rind, ginger and cinnamon sticks. In small square of cheesecloth, tie up star anise,

cloves, cardamom and peppercorns; add to pan and bring to boil. Boil for 5 minutes.

● Drain pears and add to pan; reduce heat and simmer, gently stirring occasionally, for 5 to 15 minutes or until pears are easily pierced with knife. With slotted spoon and letting excess liquid drip off, transfer pears to three 2-cup (500 mL) canning jars.

● Bring syrup to rolling boil; boil, skimming off foam, for 10 to 12 minutes or until reduced to 3 cups (750 mL). Strain over pears in jars, leaving 1/2-inch (1 cm) headspace. Discard lemon rind and ginger; divide cinnamon among jars. Untie cheesecloth bag; divide spices among jars.

● Run narrow spatula between pears and jar to release any air bubbles; add more liquid if necessary to re-establish headspace. Seal with prepared discs and bands. Process in boiling water bath for 10 minutes. (See Preserving Basics, p. 76.) Let cool. Makes 6 cups (1.5 L).

TIP: If desired, apple juice can be substituted for the red wine; reduce the sugar to 2 cups (500 mL) and the boiling time for syrup to 5 to 8 minutes.

Light Berry Currant Jam ▲

4 cups	strawberries	1 L
3 cups	raspberries	750 mL
2 cups	blueberries	500 mL
1-1/2 cups	red currants	375 mL
1	can frozen apple juice concentrate, thawed	1
3/4 cup	granulated sugar	175 mL

● In large heavy nonaluminum pot, mash strawberries with potato masher. Add raspberries, blueberries and red currants; lightly crush. Stir in apple juice concentrate, making sure pan is no more than half full.

● Bring to boil over medium heat; reduce heat, cover and simmer for 10 minutes. Stir in sugar and return to boil over high heat; boil vigorously, stirring almost constantly, for 25 minutes or until at soft set stage.

● (To test for setting point, drop 1/2 tsp/ 2 mL hot mixture onto 1 chilled plate and let cool. Return to freezer for 2 minutes. Tilt plate; if mixture flows slowly, it is softly set. If it is syrupy, continue to boil, repeating test every few minutes with clean chilled plate.)

● Remove from heat. Using metal spoon, stir and skim off foam for 5 minutes. Pour into five 1-cup (250 mL) canning jars, leaving 1/4-inch (5 mm) headspace. Seal with prepared discs and bands. Process in boiling water bath for 10 minutes. (See Preserving Basics, p. 76.) Let cool. Store for up to 6 months. Makes 5 cups (1.25 L).

Strawberries and currants are not always available at the same time, so during strawberry season, freeze enough berries for this jewel-colored jam to team up with the currants later in the year.

Per tbsp (15 mL): about
- 25 calories
- trace fat
- trace protein
- 6 g carbohydrate

Raspberry Pear Jam

This is a jam to make in cold weather. One sniff as it boils and you'll remember August and the fragrance of fresh raspberries.

Per tbsp (15 mL): about
- 40 calories
- trace protein
- trace fat
- 10 g carbohydrate

3	pkg (each 10 oz/300 g) frozen raspberries	3
3 cups	diced peeled pears	750 mL
1 tbsp	lemon juice	15 mL
1	pkg (1.7 oz/49 g) light fruit pectin crystals	1
4-1/2 cups	granulated sugar	1.125 L

● Thaw and drain raspberries, reserving juice. Crush berries to make 2 cups (500 mL). Add enough juice to make 3 cups (750 mL).

● In large heavy saucepan, combine crushed raspberries, pears and lemon juice. Combine pectin crystals with 1/4 cup (50 mL) of the sugar; stir into fruit mixture. Bring to full rolling boil over high heat, stirring constantly; stir in remaining sugar. Cook, stirring constantly, until in full rolling boil that cannot be stirred down. Boil, stirring, for 1 minute.

● Remove from heat. Using metal spoon, stir and skim off foam for 5 minutes. Pour into seven 1-cup (250 mL) canning jars, leaving 1/4-inch (5 mm) headspace. Seal with prepared discs and bands. Process in boiling water bath for 10 minutes. (See Preserving Basics, p. 76.) Let cool. Makes about 7 cups (1.75 L).

Cranberry Pear Jam

"Softly set" best describes this versatile jam — terrific on toast and scones, delectable with turkey, duck and chicken — hot or cold!.

Per tbsp (15 mL): about
- 45 calories
- 0 g protein
- 0 g fat
- 11 g carbohydrate

6 cups	cranberries	1.5 L
3 cups	diced peeled pears	750 mL
1 tsp	coarsely grated lemon rind	5 mL
2 tbsp	lemon juice	25 mL
4-1/2 cups	granulated sugar	1.125 L

● In large pot, combine cranberries, pears and lemon rind and juice; bring to boil. Cover and cook over medium heat, stirring occasionally, for 12 to 15 minutes or until tender.

● Stir in sugar and return to boil over high heat; boil vigorously, stirring constantly, for 3 to 5 minutes or until at soft set stage. Test for setting point (see box, below).

● Remove from heat. Using metal spoon, stir and skim off foam for 5 minutes. Pour into six 1-cup (250 mL) canning jars, leaving 1/4-inch (5 mm) headspace. Seal with prepared discs and bands. Process in boiling water bath for 10 minutes. (See Preserving Basics, p. 76.) Let cool. Makes 6 cups (1.5 L).

TO TEST FOR SETTING POINT
● To test for setting point, drop 1/2 tsp (2 mL) hot mixture onto 1 chilled plate and let cool. Return to freezer for 2 minutes. Tilt plate; if mixture flows slowly, it is softly set. If it is syrupy, continue to boil, repeating test every few minutes with clean chilled plate.

Apple Spread

2 lb	red-skinned apples (about 8)	1 kg
1-1/2 cups	water	375 mL
1-1/2 cups	granulated sugar	375 mL
1/2 tsp	cinnamon	2 mL
Pinch	ground cloves	Pinch

● Without peeling or coring, chop apples. In heavy saucepan, bring apples and water to boil; reduce heat, cover and simmer, stirring occasionally, for about 30 minutes or until very soft. Push through food mill or sieve; return to clean saucepan.

● Add sugar, cinnamon and cloves; simmer, stirring often, for about 35 minutes or until wooden spoon scraped across bottom of pan leaves hollow that takes 3 seconds to fill in.

● Spoon into sterilized jars, leaving 1/4-inch (5 mm) headspace. Seal and refrigerate for up to 1 month. Makes about 3 cups (750 mL).

N*o, this is not apple butter (a dark-brown apple spread that includes boiled-down apple cider); it's a delicate, fresh, apple-tasting toast topper.*

Per tbsp (15 mL): about
- 35 calories
- 0 g fat
- 0 g protein
- 8 g carbohydrate

Rhubarb Orange Conserve

1	orange, thinly sliced	1
4	thin slices lemon	4
1 cup	water	250 mL
5-1/2 cups	chopped rhubarb (1/2-inch/1 cm pieces), about 1-1/2 lb (750 kg)	1.375 L
3-1/2 cups	granulated sugar	875 mL
1 cup	golden raisins	250 mL

● In small saucepan, combine orange, lemon and water; cover and cook over low heat for 20 to 30 minutes or until peel is tender and translucent.

● In large heavy pot, stir together orange mixture, rhubarb, sugar and raisins; bring to full rolling boil, stirring constantly. Boil vigorously, stirring constantly, for about 15 minutes or until at setting point (see box, p. 82).

● Remove from heat. Using metal spoon, stir and skim off foam for 5 minutes. Pour into four 1-cup (250 mL) canning jars, leaving 1/4-inch (5 mm) headspace. Seal with prepared discs and bands. Process in boiling water bath for 10 minutes. (See Preserving Basics, p. 76.) Makes 4 cups (1 L).

I*f you're a fan of the rhubarb, wait till you taste what a hit of orange and lemon can do to this springtime favorite.*

Per tbsp (15 mL): about
- 52 calories
- 0 g fat
- trace protein
- 14 g carbohydrate

Brandied Peaches

1 tbsp	ascorbic acid color keeper crystals	15 mL
6 lb	peaches	2.7 kg
3 cups	granulated sugar	750 mL
1-3/4 cups	brandy	425 mL

● In bowl, dissolve ascorbic acid in 8 cups (2 L) water. Peel, halve and pit peaches, adding to bowl as you work.

● Meanwhile, in saucepan, stir together sugar and 2-1/4 cups (550 mL) water; bring to boil. Reduce heat and simmer gently until dissolved.

● Drain peaches; pat dry. Pack firmly, cavity side down, into seven 2-cup (500 mL) canning jars. Pour 1/4 cup (50 mL) of the hot sugar syrup into each, then 1/4 cup (50 mL) brandy. Pour enough of the remaining syrup into each jar to leave 1/2-inch (1 cm) headspace.

● Run narrow spatula between peaches and jar to release any air bubbles; add more liquid if necessary to re-establish headspace. Seal with prepared discs and bands. Process in boiling water bath for 10 minutes. (See Preserving Basics, p. 76.) Makes 14 cups (3.5 L).

C*hase the winter blues away with a generous serving of these sunny peaches in brandy syrup. They're especially cheering over ice cream or frozen yogurt.*

Per serving of peach half plus 2 tbsp (25 mL) liquid: about
- 120 calories
- trace fat
- 1 g protein
- 27 g carbohydrate

Plum Conserve

2	small navel oranges, cut in chunks	2
1 cup	water	250 mL
8 cups	sliced pitted plums (3 lb/1.5 kg)	2 L
5 cups	granulated sugar	1.25 L
3/4 cup	raisins	175 mL
2 tbsp	lemon juice	25 mL

● In food processor or food grinder using coarse blade, chop or grind oranges until in medium-fine pieces.

● In shallow heavy wide saucepan, bring oranges and water to boil; cover, reduce heat and simmer gently for 15 minutes or until softened. Add plums, stirring to coat well; return to simmer, stirring often. Cover, reduce heat to low and simmer for about 10 minutes or until plums are softened and start to release juices.

● Stir in sugar, raisins and lemon juice; bring to full rolling boil, stirring constantly. Boil vigorously, stirring constantly, for about 15 minutes or until at soft set stage.

● (To test for setting point, drop 1/2 tsp/ 2 mL hot mixture onto 1 chilled plate and let cool. Return to freezer for 2 minutes. Tilt plate; if mixture flows slowly, it is softly set. If it is syrupy, continue to boil, repeating test every few minutes with clean chilled plate.)

● Remove from heat. Using metal spoon, stir and skim off foam for 5 minutes. Pour into seven 1-cup (250 mL) canning jars, leaving 1/4-inch (5 mm) headspace. Seal with prepared discs and bands. Process in boiling water bath for 10 minutes. (See Preserving Basics, p. 76.) Makes about 7 cups (1.75 L).

Microwave Light Raspberry Cherry Jam

2 tbsp	light fruit pectin crystals	25 mL
1-3/4 cups	granulated sugar	425 mL
1-1/2 cups	crushed raspberries (3 cups/750 mL whole)	375 mL
1-1/4 cups	pitted sour cherries	300 mL

● Mix pectin crystals with 1/4 cup (50 mL) of the sugar. In 16-cup (4 L) microwaveable bowl, combine raspberries, cherries and pectin mixture. Microwave, uncovered, at High for 5 to 8 minutes or until at full rolling boil, stirring once.

● Stir in remaining sugar; microwave, uncovered, at High for 4 to 6 minutes or until returned to full rolling boil, stirring twice. Microwave at High for 1 minute.

● Fill and seal sterilized jars; store in refrigerator for up to 1 month. Makes 3 cups (750 mL).

MAKING JAM IN THE MICROWAVE

Use the size of microwave measure or bowl specified, because jams boil over easily. Make small-batch recipes as instructed; don't double them. Stir at recommended intervals to dissolve sugar and distribute heat.

Light Strawberry Banana Jam

5 cups	strawberries	1.25 L
1 cup	mashed bananas	250 mL
2 tbsp	lemon juice	25 mL
1	pkg (1.7 oz/49 g) light fruit pectin crystals	1
2 cups	granulated sugar	500 mL

● In heavy nonaluminum pot, mash strawberries with potato masher. Stir in bananas and lemon juice, making sure pan is no more than half full.

● Combine pectin crystals with 1/4 cup (50 mL) of the sugar; stir into strawberry mixture. Bring to full rolling boil over high heat, stirring constantly; stir in remaining sugar. Cook, stirring constantly, until fruit mixture is in full rolling boil that cannot be stirred down. Boil, stirring, for 1 minute.

● Remove from heat. Using metal spoon, stir and skim off foam for 5 minutes. Pour into five 1-cup (250 mL) canning jars, leaving 1/4-inch (5 mm) headspace. Seal with prepared discs and bands. Process in boiling water bath for 10 minutes. (See Preserving Basics, p. 76.) Let cool. Makes 5 cups (1.25 L).

Bananas add a smooth consistency and honeylike sweetness to this lightened-up strawberry jam.

Per tbsp (15 mL): about
- 30 calories
- trace fat
- trace protein
- 7 g carbohydrate

TIP: The specified amount of sugar is crucial to consistency. Do not reduce it or replace it with artificial sweeteners.

THE PICK OF THE STRAWBERRY CROP

Whether strawberries are from a pick-your-own farm or the local supermarket, here's how to get the maximum quality.

● Look for glossy, firm fruit with bright-green hulls attached. Depending on variety, berries can vary from bright to dark red.

● When picking, put berries in shallow containers so they aren't crushed. Avoid large baskets or pails.

● At home, sort through berries and remove any damaged ones to use right away.

● Arrange unwashed berries, with hulls on, in single layer on tray; cover with paper towel and refrigerate for up to three days.

● Just before serving, wash berries gently under cool water; pat dry and remove hulls.

Dried Cranberries

Sweetened dried cranberries are nifty additions to granola, muffins and scones.

Per 1/4 cup (50 mL): about
- 140 calories
- trace protein
- 36 g carbohydrate
- trace fat

TIP: Small berries may dry out in less than three hours; in the last hour, remove individual berries when dry.

2/3 cup	water	150 mL
1/2 cup	granulated sugar	125 mL
1	pkg (12 oz/340 g) fresh cranberries	1

● In small saucepan, stir water with sugar; cook over medium-high heat, stirring, for 2 to 3 minutes or until sugar is completely dissolved.

● Wash and pat dry cranberries. Using sharp knife, cut each berry in half. In bowl, stir berries with syrup; let stand for at least 1 hour or overnight.

● Spread on lightly greased baking sheet, reserving syrup. Bake in 175°F (80°C) oven for 1 hour.

● Drizzle with reserved syrup, stirring to coat; bake for 2 hours or until wrinkled and dehydrated but still soft and pliable. Transfer to cool baking sheet, plate or board; let stand, uncovered, in cool, dry place for 12 hours. Wrap tightly; refrigerate or freeze for up to 2 months. Makes 1-1/4 cups (300 mL).

PUT A FREEZE ON SUMMER

Freezing Fruit
● Berries, grapes and rhubarb freeze well without sugar; tray-freeze to prevent clumping and to facilitate measuring.

● Pack other fruits with some sugar to preserve flavor, color and texture.

● To prevent discoloration of fruits such as peaches, your best buy is ascorbic acid (vitamin C), available in drugstores or health food stores. You can also use packaged mixes of ascorbic acid and sugar.

● To use ascorbic acid, dissolve 1/4 tsp (1 mL) crystals or 1,000 mg in tablet form in 1/4 cup (50 mL) cold water. Sprinkle over 4 cups (1 L) prepared fruit; mix gently, then add sugar as directed. Toss gently.

Tray-Freezing
● Spread prepared fruit in single layer on tray or baking sheet; freeze, uncovered, for about 1 hour or until firm. Bag and return to freezer.

Packing and Storing
● Pack fruit in measured quantities suitable for family servings or recipe requirements.

● Use only bags or containers designed for freezing. Avoid freezer burn (food dehydration) by removing as much air as possible from packaging; suck out air with a straw before closing bag tightly.

● Label packages: include type of food, date and volume or weight measure.

● Freeze produce quickly, making sure your freezer can hold the amount you bought. Freeze no more than 2 to 3 lb (1 to 1.5 kg) fresh food per cubic foot of space at a time.

● Place food packages 1 inch (2.5 cm) apart in freezer to allow for air circulation, for 4 hours. Once frozen, stack packages closely together.

● Tape a list to the outside of your freezer so you can keep track of what you've frozen and when.

Preparing Fruit for Freezing
Apricots
● Halve or quarter; pit.

● Combine fruit and dissolved ascorbic acid. Mix in 3/4 cup (175 mL) granulated sugar for every 4 cups (1 L) fruit. Pack.

Blueberries, blue grapes, blackberries, cranberries, currants, gooseberries, raspberries, saskatoons
● Stem. Wipe with damp towel or wash only if necessary. Leave seedless grapes whole: halve and pit grapes with seeds.

● Tray-freeze; pack.

Nectarines, peaches
● Halve, pit and slice nectarines. Blanch peaches for 30 to 60 seconds; refresh in ice water. Peel, pit and slice.

● Combine fruit and dissolved ascorbic acid. Mix in 3/4 cup (175 mL) granulated sugar for every 4 cups (1 L) fruit. Pack.

Plums
● Halve and pit.

● Mix in 3/4 cup (175 mL) granulated sugar for every 4 cups (1 L) fruit. Pack.

Rhubarb
● Cut stalks into 1-inch (2.5 cm) lengths.

● Tray-freeze; pack.

Sour cherries
● Stem and pit.

● Mix in 1 cup (250 mL) granulated sugar for every 4 cups (1 L) fruit. Pack.

Strawberries
● Wipe with damp towel or wash only if necessary. Hull.

● Tray-freeze; pack.

Peach Leather

4 cups	chopped (unpeeled) peaches or nectarines (about 5)	1 L
2 tbsp	granulated sugar	25 mL

● In blender or food processor, purée peaches with sugar until smooth to make about 3 cups (750 mL).

● MICROWAVE METHOD: Pour purée into large microwaveable bowl; microwave at High, stirring occasionally, for 15 minutes or until thickened and reduced by half. Line 10-inch (25 cm) microwaveable pie plate with plastic wrap. Spread 1/4 cup (50 mL) of the purée in 6-inch (15 cm) circle in center. Microwave at Medium (50%) for about 6 minutes or until no longer sticky in center. Repeat with remaining purée.

● OVEN METHOD: Pour purée into deep saucepan and bring to boil; reduce heat and simmer, stirring often, for 30 minutes or until reduced by half. Let cool to room temperature. Line 2 baking sheets with foil; grease foil. Spread 1/4 cup (50 mL) of the purée into each of six 6-inch (15 cm) circles on foil. Bake in 175°F (80°C) oven for 2 to 3 hours or until no longer sticky in center, rotating pan halfway through.

● BOTH METHODS: Transfer fruit leather on plastic wrap or foil to rack; let stand, uncovered, at room temperature overnight or until completely dry. Roll up in plastic wrap and store in refrigerator for up to 2 weeks. Makes 6 servings.

*C*hewy, textured peach *leather has an intense flavor.*

Per serving: about
- 50 calories
- trace fat
- 1 g protein
- 12 g carbohydrate

True-Blue Blueberry Sauce

8 cups	blueberries	2 L
2-1/2 cups	apple juice	625 mL
1 tbsp	finely grated lemon rind	15 mL
1-1/4 cups	granulated sugar	300 mL
2/3 cup	corn syrup	150 mL
1/4 cup	lemon juice	50 mL

● In large heavy nonaluminum pot, combine blueberries, apple juice and lemon rind; cook over medium heat, stirring and mashing berries (but leaving a few whole), for about 15 minutes or until boiling. Gradually stir in sugar, then corn syrup and lemon juice. Return to boil; boil, stirring often, for 15 minutes.

● Remove from heat. Pour into four 2-cup (500 mL) canning jars, leaving 1/4-inch (5 mm) headspace. Seal with prepared discs and bands. Process in boiling water bath for 10 minutes. (See Preserving Basics, p. 76.) Makes about 8 cups (2 L).

A glossy dessert sauce is a cook's best friend. Use this delicious one over ice cream or frozen yogurt, or spoon onto pancakes, blintzes or waffles.

Per 2 tbsp (25 mL): about
- 40 calories
- trace fat
- trace protein
- 10 g carbohydrate

Strawberry Sundae Topping

This tasty, not-too-sweet sauce is particularly delectable over ice cream.

Per 1/2 cup (125 mL): about
- 140 calories
- 1 g protein
- trace fat
- 35 g carbohydrate

8 cups	halved strawberries	2 L
1/4 cup	water	50 mL
1 tbsp	coarsely grated orange rind	15 mL
1 cup	granulated sugar	250 mL
1/2 cup	corn syrup	125 mL
1/2 cup	orange juice	125 mL

● In large heavy saucepan, combine strawberries, water and orange rind; bring to boil over medium heat. Reduce heat to medium-low; cover and simmer for 10 minutes. Stir in sugar, corn syrup and orange juice; return to boil and boil, uncovered, for 10 minutes, stirring often.

● Pour into six 1-cup (250 mL) canning jars, leaving 1/4-inch (5 mm) headspace. Seal with prepared discs and bands. Process in boiling water bath for 10 minutes. (See Preserving Basics, p. 76.) Makes 6 cups (1.5 L).

Rhubarb Nectar

This is so refreshing that you'll want to have it on hand all summer long. It will keep refrigerated for one week, or longer if processed in a boiling water bath.

Per 1/2 cup (125 mL): about
- 150 calories
- 1 g protein
- trace fat
- 38 g carbohydrate

10 cups	chopped rhubarb (about 3 lb/1.5 kg)	2.5 L
3 cups	water	750 mL
1	strip each orange and lemon rind	1
2 cups	granulated sugar	500 mL

● In large saucepan, combine rhubarb, water and orange and lemon rinds; bring to boil over high heat. Reduce heat to medium-low; cover and simmer for 10 minutes or until rhubarb is broken up.

● Strain through cheesecloth-lined strainer into clean saucepan. Stir in sugar and bring to boil.

● Pour into six 1-cup (250 mL) canning jars, leaving 1/4-inch (5 mm) headspace. Seal with prepared discs and bands. Process in boiling water bath for 5 minutes. (See Preserving Basics, p. 76.) Shake or stir before using. Makes 6 cups (1.5 mL).

DRIED APPLES

Drying your own apples when the harvest is bountiful and the prices are low lends to terrific gift giving and delicious baking all year round. Dried apples are delicious in compotes, muffins and loaves. Pack them in decorative cellophane bags and tie with a raffia bow that holds a handwritten card for your favorite apple recipe.

● Peel and core 6 large apples; slice crosswise into 1/4-inch (5 mm) thick rings. Place about one-third of the slices in single layer in shallow dish. Dissolve 2 tbsp (25 mL) ascorbic acid color keeper crystals in 1/3 cup (75 mL) water; pour over apples, turning to coat. Let stand for 3 minutes. Transfer apples to plate, shaking excess liquid

back into dish. Repeat with remaining apples.
● Thread apple rings onto heavy kitchen strings. Tie string ends between two anchoring locations in cool dry place to make "clothesline"; space apples 1/2 inch (1 cm) apart. Let dry for at least 2 days or for up to 4 days or until apples are leathery, still pliable and no

moisture remains on fingertips when apples are touched.
● Transfer to resealable plastic bag. Store in cool, dry place for up to 6 months. Makes 3 cups (750 mL).

Per 1 cup (250 mL): about
- 225 calories ● 1 g protein
- 1 g fat ● 58 g carbohydrate
- very high source of fiber

Lemon, Lime and Rosemary Jelly

4	limes	4
2	lemons	2
2-1/2 cups	cold water	625 mL
6	sprigs (4 inches/ 10 cm long) fresh rosemary	6
3-3/4 cups	granulated sugar	925 mL
1	pkg (2.8 oz/85 mL) liquid pectin	1

● Thinly slice 1 each of the limes and lemons. Squeeze remaining fruit to make about 1/2 cup (125 mL) juice.

● In saucepan, combine water, lime and lemon slices, juice and 2 of the rosemary sprigs; bring to boil. Reduce heat and simmer for about 10 minutes or until reduced to 2 cups (500 mL). Strain through dampened jelly bag (see Tip below).

● Transfer to clean saucepan. Stir in sugar; bring to full rolling boil over high heat, stirring constantly. Add liquid pectin; boil vigorously, stirring constantly, for 1 minute. Remove from heat. Using metal spoon, skim off foam.

● Divide remaining rosemary sprigs among four sterilized 1-cup (250 mL) jars; pour in jelly, leaving 1/8-inch (3 mm) headspace. Seal and refrigerate for up to 2 months. Makes 4 cups (1 L).

TIP: For a jelly bag, you need porous yet tightly woven fabric, such as unbleached cotton. Before using, rinse in water and wring dry. Line sieve suspended over large measuring cup. Pour in mixture; tie corners of fabric to form pouch. Let drip at room temperature.

S*erve this tart and sweet jelly with lamb, chicken or fish. Or drizzle it over cheesecake for a crisp citrus accent.*

Per tbsp (15 mL): about
● 60 calories ● 0 g protein
● 0 g fat ● 16 g carbohydrate

Raspberry Vinegar

6 cups	frozen raspberries (or two 10 oz/300 g pkg)	1.5 L
3 cups	white wine vinegar or rice vinegar	750 mL
2 tsp	granulated sugar	10 mL
	Raspberries (fresh or thawed)	

● In food processor, chop together frozen raspberries, vinegar and sugar. Transfer to large microwaveable bowl or saucepan; cover and microwave at Medium-High (70%) for 7 minutes, or heat on stove top over medium heat for 10 minutes, or until steaming. Let cool.

● Refrigerate for 12 hours, stirring occasionally. Strain through fine nylon sieve into bowl, pressing to extract liquid.

● Line funnel with coffee filter or rinsed double-thickness fine cheesecloth; place in clean, dry bottle. Pour in raspberry liquid; let stand until completely filtered, topping up filter and changing to new bottles as necessary, about 8 hours.

● Add about 3 raspberries per bottle; seal with cork. Store in cool, dark, dry spot. Makes about 5 cups (1.25 L).

M*aking fruit vinegars is relatively easy, and so useful. With this one you can brighten a bowl of berries or add zip to a salad, or splash it into a pan when making a quick sauce for chicken or pork.*

Per tbsp (15 mL): about
● 4 calories ● trace protein
● 0 g fat ● 1 g carbohydrate

The Contributors

Joanne Yolles

Photography Credits

FRED BIRD: pages 31, 54, 73, 85.

DOUGLAS BRADSHAW: pages 7, 8, 21, 32, 51, 78, 81.

CHRISTOPHER CAMPBELL: pages 48, 75, 77.

PETER CHOU: page 40.

VINCENT NOGUCHI: page 42.

CURTIS TRENT: photo of Elizabeth Baird and Test Kitchen staff.

MICHAEL WARING: pages 19, 26, 37, 44, 46, 57, 61, 67, 70.

ROBERT WIGINGTON: pages 4, 10, 13, 15, 17, 20, 23, 24, 34, 38, 45, 52, 56, 62, 63, 64, 82, 87.

KATE WILLIAMS: page 59.

In the Test Kitchen. From left: Kate Gammal, Susan Van Hezewijk, Donna Bartolini (Test Kitchen manager), Jennifer MacKenzie, Daphna Rabinovitch (associate food director) and Elizabeth Baird (food director). Absent from photo: Heather Howe and Emily Richards.

Special Thanks

Susan Antonacci, Julia Armstrong, Donna Bartolini

Hugh Brewster, Kate Bush, Cate Cochran

Bonnie Baker Cowan, Albert Cummings, Susan Doherty-Hannaford

Carol Ferguson, Ruth Gangbar, Olga Goncalves

Tina Gaudino, Heather Howe, Sharon Joliat

Maggi Jones, Michael Killingsworth, Caren King

Jennifer MacKenzie, Jennifer McLagan, Robert Murray

Wanda Nowakowska, Daphna Rabinovitch, Beverley Renahan

Lucie Richard, Emily Richards, Bridget Sargeant

Barbara Selley, Gord Sibley, Beverley Sotolov

Claire Stancer, Shelly Tauber, Olga Truchan

Susan Van Hezewijk, Dale Vokey, Janet Walkinshaw

Index

The Best Things in the Kitchen are the COOK'S OWN!

Vegetables — Elizabeth Baird

Chicken — Elizabeth Baird

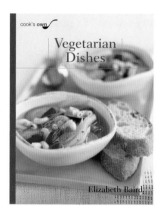
Vegetarian Dishes — Elizabeth Baird

Fish and Seafood — Elizabeth Baird

Fruit — Elizabeth Baird

Easy Cooking — Elizabeth Baird

Pasta — Elizabeth Baird

Muffins and More — Elizabeth Baird

Cookies and Squares — Elizabeth Baird

One-Dish Meals — Elizabeth Baird

Barbecue — Elizabeth Baird

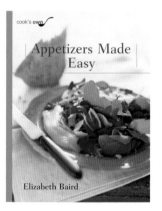
Appetizers Made Easy — Elizabeth Baird

Breads and Pizzas — Elizabeth Baird

Weekend Pleasures — Elizabeth Baird

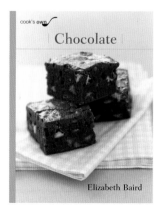
Chocolate — Elizabeth Baird

Quick Suppers — Elizabeth Baird